Inc.
MAGAZINE

301
GREAT
CUSTOMER SERVICE
IDEAS

from America's
Most Innovative Small Companies

INTRODUCTION BY HARVEY MACKAY

EDITED BY NANCY ARTZ

Book design by Cynthia M. Davis/Cambridge Prepress.
Original design by Robert Lesser.

Portions of this book were originally published in *Inc.* magazine.
For information about purchasing back issues of *Inc.* magazine,
please call 617-248-8426.

This publication is designed to provide accurate and
authoritative information in regard to the subject matter
covered. It is sold with the understanding that the publisher
is not engaging in rendering legal, accounting, or other
professional service. If legal advice or other expert assistance
is required, the services of a competent professional should
be sought.

This book may be purchased in bulk at discounted rates for
sales promotions, premiums, or fund raising. Custom books
and book excerpts of this publication are available. Write:
Inc. Business Resources
Attn: Custom Publishing Sales Dept.
38 Commercial Wharf
Boston, MA 02110-3883
or call 1-800-394-1746.

Library of Congress Catalog Number: 97-72582

ISBN 1-880394-33-2

First Edition

1 2 3 4 5 6 7 8 9 10

www.inc.com/products

301
GREAT
CUSTOMER SERVICE
IDEAS

Business is a team sport. Writing this book was no exception. A talented team conducted original research to write more than half of the material in *301 Great Customer Service Ideas*. Many of the ideas originated in the hundreds of applications submitted each year for the *Inc.* Positive Performer Awards. These prestigious awards recognize growing businesses that offer exemplary service to customers. Other ideas were culled from the best service stories in *Inc.* magazine from the last several years.

I am indebted to my husband, Dudley Greeley, for his labors as idea generator, researcher, writer, reviser, and sounding board. My thanks go to him and to my daughter, Dana Artz, for their support and patience during the intense process of writing a book. I would also like to thank the many friends and family members who offered ideas for the book.

I sincerely appreciate the stellar efforts of those who researched and wrote new customer-service ideas: Alessandra Bianchi, Richard Bilodeau, Scott Choquette, and Teri Lammers Prior. Audra Mulhearn deserves recognition for her dedication and skill in selecting material from the *Inc.* magazine archives.

A heartfelt thank-you goes to the hundreds of business owners and managers who returned phone calls and E-mail to share their stories. I also appreciate the work of the writers and editors of the *Inc.* material: Margherita Altobelli, Alessandra Bianchi, Leslie Brokaw, Christopher Caggiano, Karen Carney, John Case, Elizabeth Conlin, Susan Donovan, Tom Ehrenfeld, Donna Fenn, Jay Finegan, Jill Andresky Fraser, David Freedman, Elyse Friedman, Robina Gangemi, George Gendron, Vera Gibbons, Susan Greco, Stephanie Gruner, Phaedra Hise, Michael Hopkins, Joshua Hyatt, Joel Kotkin, Nancy Lyons, Joshua Macht, Robert Mamis, Martha Mangelsdorf, Cheryl McManus, Anne Murphy, Teri Lammers Prior,

Tom Richman, Sarah Schafer, Ellyn Spragins, Edward Welles, David Whitford, and Stephanie Zacharek.

Thanks to the *Inc.* Business Resources team who brought the book to life: editorial director Bradford W. Ketchum, Jr., who gave me the chance to write the book; copy editors Jacqueline Lapidus and Audra Mulhearn, who made the prose sparkle; fact checkers Simeon R. Ketchum and Sara Fraser, who made every story accurate; and product director Jan Spiro and product manager Kate Titus, who managed the production details.

I am also grateful to *Inc.* executive editor Jeffrey Seglin, who conceived the idea of collecting the best from *Inc.*; and creative director Cynthia M. Davis and associate art director Kathleen Edwards of Cambridge Prepress Services, for their continued excellence in shaping the 301 series look. And, finally, special thanks to *Inc.* Business Resources managing editor Sarah J. Fernberger, who orchestrated the book's creation, for her wisdom throughout the process.

—*Nancy Artz*
Editor
Portland, Maine

Editor's Note: *Nancy Artz, Ph.D., is an associate professor of business administration at the University of Southern Maine.*

A management guru offered to do some envelope business with me. Here's how he operates.

"Let's say you're in banking. You've got the biggest, most efficient, most technologically advanced operation of any bank in your fed district. The problem is your image. The focus groups show that you're perceived as cold, remote, and impersonal. If you don't do something, you'll lose business. So, what do we recommend?"

He pulled out a piece of stationery.

The company logo looked as if it were written in longhand, and next to it was a pen-and-ink drawing. It showed a big cowboy and a little cowboy. They were walking down a dusty trail, with the big cowboy leading the little cowboy by the hand. A caption under the drawing read, "Helping the West grow one step at a time."

"Just us friendly folks, right?" he continued. "Even though you can't get a live human being on the phone in less than 10 minutes unless you've got at least a $100,000 free credit balance.

"Now, let's say you're in the same state, but it's a one-bank outfit where you can barely find an abacus, much less a computer. Do you think customers want to do business in a place that looks as if it hasn't changed since Jesse James knocked it over?"

He took out another piece of stationery from his bag of tricks. It looked like a printout. The company logo was set in computer-style typeface.

"Notice the name of the bank," he continued. "It used to be State Bank of Hicksville. Now it's SBH Corporation. And they've installed one of those computerized phone operations. Lots of recorded messages. Cutting-edge stuff. What do you think?"

I passed on the chance to sell some envelopes to this gentleman.

And you will not find his approach to customer service among the 301 ideas set forth here. It wouldn't even have made the cut if there had been *601* great customer-service ideas.

What Nancy Artz offers, along with fresh and practical ways to tune in to your customers' needs, is a real respect and concern for the customer as an individual. No smoke and mirrors. No how-to-fake-it stuff.

These ideas work, too. I know. I've used many of them myself. Of course, I have my own favorite. I send copies of my books—inscribed with a personal message—to my customers. And because I have come to realize that I haven't cornered the market on the world's collective wisdom, I also often send out copies of *Inc.*'s books. I can't autograph those—I didn't write them—but at least I think I can recognize when someone else has a good idea.

Which brings me back to *301 Great Customer Service Ideas*.

I've always believed that customer service must be a strategy that is practiced in every aspect of your business—by everyone in your company. You must hire the right people, keep your suppliers happy, recognize and reward your employees—and always deliver more than you promise. Every customer should feel like your only customer.

Here are 301 smart, honest, and practical ways to connect with your customers.

Nancy, please don't forget to send me an autographed copy.

Harvey Mackay is the author of Swim with the Sharks without Being Eaten Alive *and his most recent book,* Dig Your Well *Before* You're Thirsty: The *Only* Networking Book You'll Ever Need.

I

"Our only rule: Use good judgment in all situations."

EXCERPT
from the
Nordstrom Employee Handbook,
Nordstrom Inc., in Seattle

Learn by Teaching

Training customer-service reps to be experts on a number of changing products is not as difficult as it sounds. Maureen Betses, service director at Harvard Business School Publishing (HBSP), in Boston, approaches this task with the philosophy that you learn the most when you teach someone else. Her customer-service reps take turns reading HBSP publications and presenting what they've learned to coworkers who deal with business customers. One rep makes a 15-minute presentation on a self-selected publication at each weekly staff meeting.

What's the benefit of **peer trainers** over traditional technical trainers? "Peer trainers have good customer knowledge," says Betses. "They are more likely to focus on how to sell the book, to whom, and when." Reps are more likely to ask questions and engage in discussion with peer trainers because they are all on the same team. Peer training is also a form of professional development for HBSP reps, because the publications they sell provide information they can use to advance their careers. In addition, Betses says, her reps are more comfortable with HBSP products, so they are more apt to suggest them to customers and thus cross-sell.

The peer presentations are one of several elements of a cross-selling program that together have increased customer-service sales 5%.

2

IDEA

Form Follows Function

If you want to provide good service, hire the right employees for the job. But what jobs are they really doing? You may need to **redefine the function of each employee** to get it right.

First Priority Group (FPG), a $33-million company that manages collision repair for corporate fleets and insurance carriers, initially emulated competitors by hiring experienced mechanics to coordinate the repair process. However, it was difficult to teach them to empathize with customers and perform follow-up service.

After losing several accounts and interviewing current, former, and prospective customers, it dawned on FPG president Michael Karpoff that his company wasn't really a car repair organization, but rather an administrative services company designed to reduce the stress and cost of the collision-repair process.

In the 10 years since the reorganization, customer satisfaction with the Plainview, N.Y., company has soared, and FPG hasn't lost a single customer because of poor service. Revenues continue to grow 25% annually. At the request of satisfied corporate customers, a comparable service for personal automobiles, now offered through affinity groups, accounts for 10% of revenues—and is growing dramatically.

360° Screening

Debra Robins, president of a San Francisco multimedia creative services firm, used to hire technicians and artists for their technical talents but was often disappointed with their customer-service skills. There had to be a better way to screen applicants.

It occurred to Robins that the best way to learn about an applicant's commitment to customers is from past customers themselves. Prospective employees are now asked to provide **references from clients** in addition to those from employers and coworkers. During reference checks, clients are asked open-ended questions about their working relationship with the applicant. Even in an era of cautious references, a picture emerges about the applicant's customer-service orientation. What is not said is often as important as what is said.

Robins, who employs 40 full-time and 20 freelance workers, has been delighted with the results. She now screens all prospective employees for their commitment to customer service.

Steering Around the Learning Curve

Most new telephone service reps are trained, given practice on a few mock calls, and sent to the phones, where supervisors supposedly give them extra attention. This training isn't enough, according to Sara Hansen, director of business development at CMC, a performance development company with call-center and training services, located in Cordova, Tenn. "We've learned from focus groups, satisfaction surveys, and exit interviews with our marketing associates that they want more support to overcome discomfort when they first hit the floor."

CMC's response was to create the Academy Bay, **a safe space for the transition from training to autonomy**. Employees in the Academy handle live calls, but a coach provides side-by-side monitoring. The coach offers feedback, reinforces positive behavior, helps the novice navigate when trouble arises, and demonstrates how to handle problem calls. "Recent trainees are awkward with new skills and scripts," says Hansen. "They need to gain confidence in a setting that recognizes the learning curve without punitive consequences."

CMC's Academy Bay focuses resources on the most vulnerable staff and shortens the learning curve. Profitability improves with shorter call-handling time, as a result of more sales per hour from both inbound and outbound calls. Best of all, employee morale is up and turnover is down 4% from pre-Academy days. This percentage may appear small, says Hansen, "but it's huge when you consider the costs of recruiting and the fact that better service results from having a higher percentage of tenured reps."

Ask, Don't Tell

Dickinson Theatres uses the motto "Ask, don't tell" to create a strong customer-service training orientation at its 39 locations. Jeff Garber, operations trainer for the 200-screen cinema chain, based in Mission, Kans., says the policy of **creating a positive environment** works in three ways:

- Managers respond with "What would *you* do?" when a front-line employee asks how to handle a customer request. "Most young people are used to being told what to do, but if you spoon-feed directions to your team members, they stop thinking for themselves. We want them to turn on their brains so they can respond positively to customers," says Garber.

- When employees interact with upset moviegoers, they ask customers what they want, rather than dictate the solution. Customer solutions are often the best.

- Employees are taught to treat each other with courtesy and respect. Instead of yelling to a coworker "I need a large popcorn!" they ask politely. "Each week we receive comments from customers who noticed how considerate team members are with one another," says Garber. "It turns a fear-driven organization into an empowering one."

The results have been dramatic for both employees and customers. Average annual employee turnover in the industry is in the high double-digits, but it was less than 3% for the first theater Dickinson opened using an intense, customer-service oriented training program. Customer satisfaction scores have risen, and local film critics have commented on the positive moviegoing experience at Dickinson Theatres.

6
IDEA

A Day in Their Shoes

Would your business do better if your employees could view the world from your customers' perspective? Yes? Then put them there with **empathy training**. Acadian Ambulance and Air Med Services, in partnership with SAA Consultants, developed an eight-hour experiential training program to sensitize its 1,100 employees to the physical and emotional needs of patients.

The $80-million medical services and transport company, based in Lafayette, La., begins sessions with a video in which older patients describe what they did in their early 20s. Staff, whose average age is 24, see that the elderly are like themselves but at a different life stage. Then employees are asked to "become" the people they serve. Some wear ear plugs to impair hearing, smear petroleum jelly on eyeglasses to impair vision, wear splints on arms or legs to simulate physical limitations, pull socks over their hands to immobilize them, and so on. With these impairments, medics perform everyday tasks ordinarily done without conscious effort, such as eating lunch. Training ends with a dialogue on how the experience relates to work and to their personal lives. Many of the paramedics became sensitized to the patients' need for emotional autonomy, which can be provided by letting patients dress themselves or have input in scheduling appointments.

"The number of complimentary letters received from patients has increased since we began empathy training five years ago," says Tommy Duhon, senior vice president of human resources. "Employees have more empathy for elderly patients and an increased appreciation for human dignity that benefits all customers."

7
IDEA

Pay 'Em to Play

Knowledgeable employees give the best service. Tuition reimbursement promotes continuing education, but not all employees want to sit in class after a full day at work, says Ariel Glassman, marketing manager for Network Software Associates (NSA). That's why the Arlington, Va., software development company began offering **financial assistance to employees who purchase job-related computer products**. The policy encourages employees to educate themselves. "People play around on their personal computers at home and learn," says Glassman.

NSA can serve its clients better, according to Glassman, if its 35 employees have a better understanding of the Internet and rapid changes in computer technology. And it's an investment in customer satisfaction, because the company stays current on both technology and customer needs. By subsidizing self-education, NSA has been able to capture 70% of the local market in just seven years.

8
IDEA

Swapping Stories

During her company's Monday morning staff meetings, Susan Groenwald, president of Barter Corp., located in Oakbrook Terrace, Ill., asks employees to **share examples of exemplary customer service** that the company has provided. Afterward, the 51 workers at the barter network, which has net revenues of $3.6 million, vote for the example they think had the greatest impact on the company's customer service. The winner gets either a cash award or bartered goods, such as use of a convenient parking spot or a gift certificate for dinner for two at a local restaurant.

"Rehashing stories gives people a better idea of what good customer service looks like," says Groenwald. "It's also a fun way to start the week." And there's an additional payoff: The meetings arm her salespeople with real-life anecdotes to use when they're wooing potential clients.

Recruit Only the Best

Whenever someone provided him with great service, Blayne Blowers made an unusual offer: He handed the person a card that read "I was impressed by your service. If you're ever looking for a job, please call me." Blowers, director of store operations for the Clean Duds laundry chain, in Des Moines, swore by the card as a screening tool.

Blowers first used cards for recruiting in 1986, when he managed 13 fast-food restaurants. The idea caught on at Clean Duds: Everyone in the home office, including the CEO, handed out the card to recruit new employees for the two company-owned stores. And the company ordered 30,000 cards for its 65 franchises.

Blowers **looked for people who were sincere and responsive**, with a friendly smile—not forced—and who seemed to enjoy serving. When cardholders called, Blowers interviewed them carefully, but he had already confirmed an important, and elusive, quality. He noted that the cards reduced the cost of bad hires and saved training time, because "customer service is the hardest thing to teach."

10

IDEA

Screen-Test Prospective Stars

To fill job vacancies, Shane Jones, CEO and owner of Ace Personnel, in Shawnee Mission, Kans., used to interview 10 people out of the hundreds who responded to his help-wanted ads. But often the bright, experienced people he hired would disappoint him because of poor customer-service skills. Jones decided to **engage the applicants in role-playing** during initial screenings over the phone.

After giving prospects a short history of Ace and its successes, he and his managers asked them what made them best for the job. "We catch them off guard," Jones says. "We see who can perform under pressure." Then candidates have to pretend to be restaurant managers, while the interviewer plays a disgruntled customer. Ace gives points for poise and imagination, subtracting points for timidity or canned answers.

If the job candidates automatically agree to refund money, that's considered a poor decision. If they offer to trade product—a coupon for a free meal—that's a good start. If they ask questions to determine why the service was unacceptable, that's best. The more questions the job candidates ask, the better. The phone screening is so efficient that Jones hires about 75% of the prospects who perform well.

11

IDEA

Teach CS101

You can make a first-rate customer-service staff out of all your employees—when you **send them back to the classroom**.

Rachel Hubka, owner of Rachel's Bus Company, in Chicago, holds workshops for her bus drivers on the fine art of asking for business. "We hold breakfast meetings to review how to thank customers and how to tell them they were a good group." Hubka printed business cards for the 120 drivers and pays them 10% commissions on every new charter client they bring in.

Lorraine Miller of Cactus & Tropicals, a $2.2-million Salt Lake City nursery, holds in-house seminars for her 30-person staff. One month the seminar is about "the plant as factory"; another month, it's about customer service. Miller uses a lot of role-playing to dramatize extreme situations, since workers need to learn how to handle customers who bring back expensive plants.

Along with pruning and mulching, certification in customer service is a requirement for field workers at $37.7-million Ruppert Landscape, in Ashton, Md. Employees study handshake delivery and practice saying "How can I help you?" Chris Davitt, vice-president of the company, explains, "When a worker is covered with dirt, the customer might not want to ask for help."

"You are only as good as the people you train."

LONEAR HEARD
president of James T. Heard Management Corp.,
a McDonald's franchisee,
in Bellflower, Calif.

IDEA

Share the Wealth

Training your employees to use the latest version of computer software is a major challenge. Meeting this challenge is critical for Diva Garza, president of International Team Consultants (ITC), a personnel services firm, based in Houston. The 5,000 temporary employees Garza sends to customers each year must have up-to-date computer skills.

Most employment agencies train their temps by using self-paced computer tutorials. Garza differentiated her firm from the competition in 1996 by investing in a state-of-the-art **training center that provides live instruction**. The result: readily available, well-trained temporary workers for ITC's customers.

Garza offers empty seats in the classroom to her customers free of charge to train their permanent employees as well. Coupons for the free training are distributed to customers on the basis of how much business they do with ITC. This value-added service doesn't cost ITC much, but it's a powerful incentive for customers to choose the agency.

"Firms can't rest on their laurels," says Garza. "They must continually find innovative ways to add value to their relationships with customers." The training has paid off for ITC: Revenues are up 28% from 1996.

13
IDEA

Spread the Word

Company presidents shouldn't be the only ones reading books and journals to learn tips for business success. "When I see a good idea, I want to share it with my employees," says Jim Johnson, president of Brandy's Automotive Repair, in Schaumburg, Ill. "Reading about success breeds success—it's contagious." Here are ways that Johnson and others encourage employees to improve themselves and their customer-service efforts.

- *Customer-service articles.* Johnson places magazine articles about customer service inside the weekly pay envelopes of the 20 customer-service staffers at Brandy's four car repair shops. Associating the articles with paychecks makes the point that customers pay their salaries—without customers, there isn't a business.

- *Motivational tapes.* Allin Companies, a 45-employee landscaping and snowplowing company, in Erie, Pa., invests in books on tape by motivational authors such as Dale Carnegie and Stephen Covey. "Crew leaders listen to the tapes when traveling from site to site—this means crew members listen too," notes president John Allin.

- *Assigned readings.* The entire management team at Service Performance, a San Jose, Calif., janitorial company, meets to discuss assigned readings. "We read four to six books per year on quality, service, or something inspirational and talk about the meaning for our company," says president Dave Pasek.

- *Headphones and daily walks.* A new program at a large Japanese corporation allows employees to take a walk in the middle of the day to listen to tapes using portable cassette players. Employees are exposed to new ideas while relieving stress through exercise.

Hire Education

Want to hire employees who give great service? Here are some **hiring and training techniques** that work well for HGO Technology, a 70-employee computer technology consulting firm, in Wheeling, W. Va.

- *Involve customers and coworkers in the hiring process.* The people who will work closely with new hires should have a voice in the decision. HGO's customers and project team members are given the opportunity to interview and approve job applicants.

- *Hire staff with advanced training in secondary areas.* HGO employees are selected for their computer expertise plus their knowledge and skills in areas such as aerospace engineering, biostatistics, accounting, technical and graphical communications, mathematics, and business administration. The added perspective helps HGO understand the needs of customers in different industries. Two government contracts, worth more than $7 million, were recently awarded to HGO as a direct result of the company's ability to offer a quality workforce with diverse talents.

- *Take prompt, corrective action when employees don't deliver superior customer service.* When necessary, terminate the employee. Go one step further and share the reason for termination with customers and employees—this reinforces the message that the company is committed to service excellence.

15
IDEA

What's at Stake?

Do you want your company to make fewer mistakes? **Explain to your employees what mistakes mean to your clients.** That's the idea behind a two-year-old training program, "The Product through the Customer's Eyes," at Solar Communications, a $60-million provider of printing and packaging for the direct marketing industry.

The two-hour training begins with a 12-item true/false pretest that asks questions about the business objectives of Solar's clients. Except for a few seasoned veterans, most workers don't know the answers, says Dr. Bill Marzano, vice-president of educational services for the Naperville, Ill., company.

To provide the answers, Marzano produced a videotape of three customers explaining how Solar's work helps them meet their marketing objectives. Workers see how mistakes have a ripple effect that can cause the whole project to grind to a halt. Employees leave training saying, "Now I understand why the codes on the materials are so important," or "Now I know why some customers have trouble getting mailing lists to us on time—they don't have a choice."

Does all this translate into better customer service? "Absolutely," says Marzano. "When employees realize what's at stake for clients, they understand the need for urgency and attention to detail. Another division, having seen our success, is making a tape tailored to its own product line."

The training program is responsible, in part, for a 25% reduction in the number of mistakes requiring a credit to Solar's customers over a two-year period.

16
IDEA

Keys to a Prized Solution

Is your company learning all it can from its mistakes? Consider the approach used by Shirley Singleton, CEO of Edgewater Technology, a $12-million custom-software solutions developer in Wakefield, Mass. Once a month, various employee teams gather for a **case study discussion**. During the discussion, a short list of humorous song titles is displayed, each one relating to a recent problem for the firm. Employees are asked to select which "song" they want to hear.

Singleton leads a spirited discussion, involving everyone in the room. Could the problem have been prevented? Is there a win-win solution? She hands a key to each employee who offers a constructive insight. At the end of the meeting, those with keys try to open a treasure chest—but only two keys can open the lock. The first person to open the chest finds $200 wrapped in golden ribbon. The second keyholder gets the booby prize: cheap steak knives, which drive home the point that success comes from being first with customers. If no key fits the lock, the prize money is doubled for the next month.

"The treasure chest may sound corny, but it works," says Singleton. "It's hard to get employees to focus on accounts other than their own. The treasure chest generates excitement and keeps people attentive at meetings. We all learn."

Short-Shrift Service

"If you don't hire people with an innate belief in serving customers, you shouldn't be surprised by mediocre service," states Mark Clement, president of Holy Cross Hospital, in Chicago. The 1,700-employee hospital uses **hiring techniques to find employees who match an ideal profile**. These techniques help to identify job candidates who exhibit attributes of service, teamwork, and high standards.

- *Values video.* Applicants are shown a 20-minute video in which hospital employees talk about working in a value-driven organization. The interviewer walks by the viewing-room door half a dozen times to note whether applicants are paying attention to the video. Those observed balancing checkbooks and filing nails don't get a second interview. Afterward, the interviewer gives an unannounced oral quiz on the video's messages.

- *Multiple interviews.* Conducted by human resources staff, department leaders, and coworkers, these include questions about previous service experiences that uncover an applicant's values and tendencies. Example: "Tell me about a situation when a patient was unhappy with waiting and how you handled it."

- *Team interviewing.* Give a joint problem-solving task to four to eight applicants, and observe how they work with one another. This is a great way to assess teamwork skills.

- *Assess success.* Three, six, and twelve months after the hire, assess how the new employee is working out, and analyze why. Clement says that this process helps human resources managers and department heads learn how to hire the right person for the position, rather than just fill job openings.

18
IDEA

The Trying Game

Joe McGarry, general manager of the Holiday Inn Arlington at Ballston, in Arlington, Va., keeps his staff trained and entertained by **playing games on company time**.

Here's how it works: McGarry modified a board game into a ballroom-sized Front Line Service Strategy Rally. The game board is projected on a 10-foot screen. Six groups of eight to 10 employees try to "delight customers" at hypothetical service opportunities determined by the roll of giant, 30-inch fuzzy dice. The draw of a card directs the groups to craft a response using one of the hotel's service strategies to create environments that are: 1) welcoming; 2) informative; 3) entertaining; and 4) caring and hassle-free; and 5) positive, but allow staff to collect payment that is due.

After five frantic minutes of deliberation, the groups present their responses using skits or oral presentations, trying to impress top management brought in as judges of the event. Every idea is recorded, and the better ones are implemented. All participants receive a pair of movie passes, candy goes to the winning table, and the hotel raffles off an expensive door prize, such as a 25-inch color TV.

According to McGarry, the hotel's low employee retention rate had been a problem. Fifty percent of employees are staying longer now, and the hotel's service scores are in the top 25% for the region.

It's the Fit That Counts

Businesses say they want new employees to share the company's commitment to customers. David Blumenthal, president and CEO of Flash Creative Management, a business technology consulting firm, in Hackensack, N.J., wonders just how successful those companies can be unless **job applicants interview with customers** as part of the hiring process. At Blumenthal's office, "Every person hired must check three company references—usually customers. When an applicant talks with our customers, what we mean by strong commitment to customers becomes real. When you join this company, you do whatever it takes to make the customer happy." Blumenthal offers other reasons for adopting the reverse reference checks.

- Prospects should know the types of clients they will be working with if they accept a position at your company. Does the candidate feel comfortable with your customer's corporate culture?

- Reverse reference checks give you the opportunity to learn more about the candidate. Follow up with your references to solicit their opinions. Did the applicant ask intelligent questions? Is this candidate acceptable to your customers? Were the candidate's strengths a good match with their needs?

- When you ask your customers for their opinions, it sends a clear message: They are important. You value their input.

- The reverse reference check assignment tests the applicant's interest in the position. If a candidate doesn't bother to contact references, he or she is not serious about the job.

20

IDEA

Building Equity in Experience

Training and retaining employees can be crucial to achieving successful service. Clean Cut, a full-service landscaping company, in Austin, Tex., accomplishes both with an innovative "stock card" program. Management trainees use the cards to record the names of experienced employees who take time to help them learn the ropes. After the trainee has been there for 10 months to three years, he or she can attain partnership status and become eligible for profit sharing. But the new partner isn't the only one who benefits. If someone has his or her name on 10% of the new partner's stock cards, every year the company writes him or her a check for an amount equal to 10% of that partner's eligible stock-card profit.

"It **rewards older employees for passing down their expertise** and wisdom to new employees," says Kevin Yeager, Clean Cut's operations manager. "This improves customer service because the newcomers learn how to deal with customers, what to say and what not to say, and how to be proactive on-site. I can testify from my own experience, as a trainee with stock cards to distribute, that others coached me on how to give better service."

As the program has grown, the larger bonuses have gotten people's attention. Workers at all levels see a direct benefit in helping new employees learn and succeed, and annual stock bonuses provide an incentive for veteran employees to stay with the firm. "This, too, improves customer service," adds Yeager. "Seasoned personnel are more knowledgeable, and we maintain continuity in the relationships we have built with clients."

21

IDEA

Healthy Home Videos

A t a service company, changes in personnel can cause the quality of service to suffer. To prevent uncomfortable and potentially aggravating situations for your customers, take a lesson from Ridgaway Philips, in Spring House, Pa., a provider of home health care to critically-ill patients. The company **videotapes its patients' on-site care routines** so that if substitutes need to fill in, they can watch the videotape and hit the ground running once they arrive at a patient's home. The videotapes detail how to enter the house, the locations of supplies, and the speech and physical therapy sessions. "For patients leaving the hospital," says Jacquelyn Moore, president and CEO of Ridgaway Philips. "we also interview the discharge nurse, who gives us tips and techniques for caring for that particular patient."

In addition to being a training aid, the videotapes provide clients with a vivid record of their progress. Kids especially love it, says Moore, whose company earns $9 million in revenues annually and employs 450 health-care providers. "Besides being a service to our clients, the tapes give us a way to show insurance companies what we are doing for patients, as they focus more on patient outcomes."

"The real key to running a successful business is to hire good people. You cannot make business decisions about competing in today's world without considering the people who have to 'buy' the concept and deliver results."

STEVE BURKHART
chairman of the board,
Advanced MicroElectronics,
in Vincennes, Ind.

Homegrown Details

Losing sales because of lousy service by shelf-stocking companies is a risk. Big retailer chains avert this risk by contracting "retail-detail" companies, which send people out to stores to make sure products are in stock and promotional displays are properly staged.

The service was too costly for Headbone Interactive, a children's multimedia publisher, located in Seattle. Walter Euyang, the operations manager, bootstrapped a solution: He **enlisted friends and family of company employees to check on displays** of Headbone products in retail outlets and touch base with the store managers.

Says Euyang, "We figured they'd work harder for us since they want to see our company succeed." The homegrown team was also much less expensive than hiring a professional firm to do the job. Overall, Euyang estimates the company cut its costs by nearly 40%. During the busy holiday season, Headbone's dedicated team performed as well as the pros. When one bookstore was all out of a hot seller, one detailer sent word of the shortage to headquarters. Inventory was shipped directly to the store, bypassing the normal distribution warehouse. "That's the type of service we couldn't depend upon from a professional firm," says Euyang.

23
IDEA

Make Exceptional Service the Standard

While standards won't substitute for passionate commitment to service excellence, they do encourage consistent behavior that satisfies customers. That's why Holy Cross Hospital, in Chicago, **outlines standards of performance** for each department and the entire organization.

The list includes eight areas in which standards are set for the entire organization: 1) phone etiquette (answer within three rings, ask for permission and wait for a response before placing a caller on hold); 2) providing directions (walk individual to destination instead of pointing, offer assistance to people who look confused); 3) personal and environmental appearance (wear name tag in an easily visible location, follow detailed rules developed by employees on clothing and grooming); 4) customer education and information (fully explain what will happen before, during, and after a procedure); 5) customer waiting (less than 10 minutes, or provide status reports at 10-minute intervals); 6) call lights (acknowledge in three minutes); 7) privacy (don't discuss patients in public areas); and 8) attitude (acknowledge people with a friendly smile and eye contact).

An employee team sets measurable standards and helps integrate them into the everyday behavior of the hospital's 1,700 employees. Each month, one standard is reviewed in department meetings. Every day, employees wear "Ask Me" buttons to engage people in conversations about standards. Mystery shopping is used to assess compliance. In addition, as a learning tool, all employees take written competency tests on these standards. Department leaders use the test results to coach individuals in areas of weakness and to decide which standards to reinforce.

Stay in Shape for Peak Demand

WinterSilks, in Middleton, Wis., knows how difficult it is to maintain high service levels when its telemarketing staff quadruples in peak season. Giving seasonal employees the same training as year-round staff doesn't solve the problem—they're still inexperienced.

"Even after new telemarketers receive two weeks of classroom training and a week of on-the-job training with a 'buddy,' they need two to three months of live experience to hone their skills," says John Reindl, vice-president of operations for the $45-million direct merchant of silk apparel. "Two months later our peak season is over, and in this industry, 40% to 60% of seasonal employees won't return the following season."

WinterSilks meets this challenge by **insourcing telemarketing work to keep most staff employed during the off-season**. Seasonal employees now stay on to take credit applications for a lawn-care provider during WinterSilks' slow season.

"Our training money no longer goes to waste, and we have an extra source of revenue," observes Reindl. "The biggest benefit is having more experienced telemarketers. Our employee retention rate has increased considerably. The telemarketers already understand our culture and service expectations, so we only need to provide two or three days of training to introduce the new season's changes." Does all this lead to better customer service? Reindl says it does. Scores on customer-satisfaction surveys have gone up since his company began the program.

25
IDEA

A Stitch in Time Saves Nine

When the office gets busy, there's a great temptation to dictate orders to the troops and skip explaining the whys of company policy. "But don't do it," urges Barbara Sealund, founder of Sealund Associates, a multimedia software training firm, based in Clearwater, Fla. "Invariably some employee will repeat a mistake that inspired a company policy, and customer service will suffer."

Sealund, a former teacher, takes time to tell her staff dramatic horror stories—missed customer deadlines, products shipped with glaring typos, and how one sales representative jumped the gun and quoted a price way too low for a project—so that **employees understand the "big picture" behind the policy**. Sealund Associates's track record is so good that the company is rarely required to bid on future work from customers. Sealund knows the additional employee training is worth the effort: 90% of her customers award her company repeat business.

"We didn't apply the principles
of Quality Management to win
the National Quality Award.
We did it to win customers."

EARNEST W. DEAVENPORT JR.
chairman and CEO of
Eastman Chemical Company,
in Kingsport, Tenn., winner of the
1993 Malcolm Baldrige National Quality Award

26
IDEA

Conversation Peace

When a customer working with several employees at a company gets two different answers to the question, "What's going on?"—who's right? At Sealund Associates, a software training firm, employees working on a project together are required to **circulate telephone notes taken when discussing the project with a customer**, to keep confusion and mistakes to a minimum. "We've done it for 13 years, and for the past several we've done it online," says Barbara Sealund, founder of the Clearwater, Fla., company. "This way even far-flung independent contractors, working off-site on a project, can tap into the log of yesterday's happenings to keep up to date."

Employees are required to download their notes into the computer system within 24 hours. Typically, they list the main points of a conversation. Speed—not polish—is what's needed at this stage of the game, and typos and incorrect grammar are overlooked. Sealund can check the projects remotely when she's traveling so that before she calls customers, she knows the status of their projects.

Sealund adds that the database serves as a useful historical tool for salespeople on the road. Since the notes document various projects, they can tap into these notes while visiting customers and brainstorm with them. Sealund Associates revenues reached $2 million in 1997, and 90% of customers give the firm repeat business.

Everybody Say Cheese

Frank Meeks, president and owner of Domino's Pizza Team Washington, a 52-store chain in the Washington, D.C., metropolitan area, has always understood the consequences of alienating customers. For employees, however, such concepts often prove abstract. So, Meeks tries to **talk real numbers with his employees and connect them with customer satisfaction**.

For example, Meeks estimates that many customers patronize his shops twice weekly, which means they spend close to $1,000 a year. Each unhappy customer therefore represents $1,000 in revenue lost annually. Actually, losses are greater still, since each unhappy customer tells about a dozen other people about his or her negative experience.

By explaining in concrete terms how every lost customer affects the bottom line, Meeks drives home the importance of keeping customers satisfied.

28
IDEA

Chill Before Serving

Employee stress and customer service are like oil and water—the two don't mix. A stressed-out employee in any industry is likely to be irritable or downright unpleasant to your customers. Even paramedics, who are trained to handle stress in emergency situations, are vulnerable, says Tommy Duhon, senior vice-president of human resources at Acadian Ambulance and Air Med Services, in Lafayette, La. What's more, for the average paramedic, day-to-day stressors may seem small, but they can accumulate and have serious physical, psychological, and behavioral consequences if the paramedics are not equipped with appropriate coping skills.

Acadian's solution is "Crackerjack," a day-long program developed in tandem with SSA Consultants. **Employees learn to reduce work-related stress** by controlling manageable situations, changing their perceptions, and accepting circumstances beyond their control. They start by examining job expectations and compare them to workplace realities to determine where conflicts exist.

The 600 employees trained so far appear to be better able to identify and cope with stress. They learn that it's okay to let others know when they have a problem. Most important, they become aware that their work is a stressor—that they need to leave it behind when they go home, to improve the quality of their family life and free time. "Paramedics with a handle on stress function crisply on the job," says Duhon. "This frees them to focus on the service they provide to customers."

II

"A customer is not an interruption of our work."

A SLOGAN
printed in huge letters
on the wall of L.L. Bean's call center,
in Freeport, Maine

29
IDEA

Peer Pressure Motivates

By making its 45 **employees responsible for setting service standards and accountable to each other** for their performance, a $1.7-million landscaping and snow plowing company, located in Erie, Pa., achieved a lofty goal—exceeding customer expectations.

Allin Companies' volunteer team of six front-line employees meets weekly to review customer feedback and employee suggestions. The team's recommendations are researched for feasibility by a five-person Leadership Council—a group composed primarily of crew foremen—responsible for setting and meeting the company's service goals.

For example, the Council decides how many complaints per month are acceptable and how long it should take to reach a new goal. Concerned about a potential increase in complaints, the Council initially rejected management's idea to accept a major new account, then it designed a training program that allowed the company to take on the new work without sacrificing service quality.

Employees know how each team performs, because customer-satisfaction survey results are published in the monthly internal newsletter. When a customer complaint arises, the employees must provide explanations—and solutions—to the customer and to peers on the Leadership Council.

President John Allin is pleased with the results: The acceptable number of complaints dropped from 10 per month to three within a year of the Council's creation, and the new goal of exceeding customer expectations has been met. "Now that pressure comes from peers," Allin says, "management doesn't have to 'beat on' employees to improve customer service. Employees motivate themselves."

30

IDEA

Workers Unite!

A group of 35 employees at World Access Service Corp., located in Richmond, Va., recently cross-trained to perform claims processing and telephone customer service. The objective was to provide one-stop shopping for customers and eliminate staffing problems caused by a widely fluctuating volume of incoming phone calls—when the phones were quiet, employees processed claims. Although they achieved these objectives, the workers didn't feel like members of a team because the group was so large. They preferred to be in small groups that worked closely together.

Pam Dufour, senior vice-president of service delivery, responded by **creating work teams**. Each team is responsible for answering incoming customer-service calls, processing claims on a timely, high-quality basis, and training new employees. Each team decides how to divide its work among its six to eight members.

Some teams take a division-of-labor approach in which the experienced member handles complicated claims, or someone who is really great on the phone answers the lion's share of calls. Other teams divide the work evenly but make daily adjustments for employee moods: Anyone needing a break from telephone work—or claims processing—is assigned to another task.

Dufour hasn't instituted formal competition between the teams, but she does post their productivity measures. Friendly competition among the teams has hiked productivity 18%. "The creation of work teams has boosted morale," says Dufour, "and happy workers provide better service."

31
IDEA

Groups Brainstorm Better

Employees can have great ideas for improving customer service, but the number of ideas placed in suggestion boxes often falls over time. To keep employee ideas flowing, Home Delivery Incontinent Supply (HDIS), a mail-order company, based in Olivette, Mo., uses a **team-based, idea-of-the-month contest**.

Once a month, the company's 35 employees gather for an hour to brainstorm improvements. Each group comprises four or five employees from different areas of the company. The composition of the group changes monthly to keep ideas fresh.

Bruce Grench, president of HDIS, assigns a discussion topic such as "How can we reduce shipping errors?" Ideas generated each month are posted. The best 10 to 15 are marked with a silver star and assigned to implementation teams. A gold star is added when the idea is implemented, which happens 95% of the time. The team that generated the "idea-of-the-month" receives a complimentary lunch or an afternoon off.

One idea-of-the-month addressed HDIS's most frequent customer complaint: "invoiced correctly but received wrong product." A redesigned invoice that left product codes visible when it was folded in the packing sleeve allowed a final check on contents and helped solve the problem. Complaints dropped from a high of 33 to an average of 13 per month.

Group brainstorming keeps team spirit strong, says Grench. And employees speak up because they know that the company listens.

Giving Credit Where It's Due

Motivated employees give good customer service. To keep his 23 employees motivated, John Zitzner, president of a $2-million, Cleveland-based software development company specializing in business form management, introduced an **affirmations bowl**. Employees at the Bradley Co. write affirmations or supportive comments when they see someone display a service-oriented attitude toward a customer or fellow employee. The affirmation cards, called "little things that cownt" (named after the company's cow mascot) are placed in the bowl.

Social recognition, says Zitzner, is as special for the writer as it is for the recipient. At the end of monthly staff meetings, Zitzner pulls about 50 cards from the bowl and reads them aloud. The writer occasionally expands upon what was written, and spontaneous applause breaks out when others add their thanks. The employee recognized on the last card drawn is given the company credit card for dinner with a guest.

Zitzner makes a point of not setting a limit on the cost of the dinner, underscoring the importance of trust in the organization. When asked, he tells employees to pick a fancy restaurant they've always wanted to try. "Setting a limit shoots away the positive feeling of the reward," says Zitzner. "The right amount to spend is what is meaningful to the employee. Going $20 over what I might set as a cap is peanuts compared to the positive motivational excitement that comes from having a good time." No one has abused the privilege, says Zitzner, and employees are motivated to give better service.

33
IDEA

Listen to the Bartender's Advice

Christopher Bear, president of the Texas School of Bartenders, in Houston, initially thought quality awards were for big companies, not for a small company like his with six employees and $430,000 in revenues. Now he knows that **competing for quality awards** provides a focal point for sustaining a commitment to quality and customer service.

"Once you get past the fear of being under the microscope, the application and award process is incredibly educational—you see the good, bad, and ugly in your business," says Bear. The Texas School of Bartending has received recognition in three of the six competitions it has entered, including the *Inc.* Positive Performer Awards and a local Houston award program modeled after the Malcolm Baldrige National Quality Award.

Time spent preparing an application is well spent, according to Bear. Involving staff in the process was key: It generated a positive attitude shift. The application questions forced Bear to examine the entire organization and look for evidence to support his assumptions. As a result, the company has made strides in implementing database technology, cross-training, and other customer-service improvements. "By placing ourselves in competitions, we challenged our goals and each other to rise to the task," says Bear. Winning recognition also boosted morale and generated publicity for the school.

34
IDEA

A Better Bonus

Low employee turnover leads to satisfied customers and repeat business. Dan Austin, director of Backcountry, an adventure vacation company, based in Bozeman, Mont., agrees. According to Austin, "Trip leaders are like fine wine—they get better with age."

Austin has developed a bonus plan that encourages his 34 trip leaders to provide exceptional service and return for employment the following season. Each time a customer comes back for another Backcountry tour, the two team leaders from the customer's last trip each receive a $25 bonus. Only current Backcountry employees are eligible for the bonus.

The beauty of this plan, according to Austin, is **awarding bonuses based on customer return rates** instead of initial sales. The bonuses go directly to the individuals who have the greatest control over the customer's experience. The bonus policy thanks them for providing a delightful customer experience, and it reinforces the trip leader's natural inclination to build personal relationships with customers. Some send postcards after the trip or phone customers when passing through their towns.

For a veteran employee, the bonus total can be substantial—as high as 10% of wages. The timing of the bonus—just before the signing of the following year's employment contract—also encourages employees to return. "Last year, 100% of our tour leaders returned," says Austin, "and 85% of customers are return customers or from direct referrals—the highest rate in the industry."

35
IDEA

Let Awards Go to Their Heads

Employee recognition programs motivate employees to deliver quality service—which leads to satisfied customers. With 100 employees to motivate, the J&S Construction Co., located in Cookeville, Tenn., created Above and Beyond the Call of Duty (ABCD) awards. This program recognizes workers praised in customer thank-you letters or employees who go the extra mile to save customers money, increase productivity, and make the workplace safer. "Recognizing employees for their extra efforts keeps them happy, and in turn they keep customers happy," says Adam Bernhardt, total quality management coordinator.

ABCD award stickers are placed on winners' hardhats, **making the awards visible to customers**. When a customer asks about the colorful stickers, the resulting discussion reinforces the company's service values and prompts customers to mention their own service needs. Accumulated stickers can be traded for a gift, and the winner is highlighted in the company newsletter, *Constructively Speaking*, which is sent to every employee, customer, and potential lead.

"Recognizing employees who work smarter, not just harder, is vital to success in this industry," says Bernhardt. The ABCD award program has paid off for J&S: In 1997, 100% of customers responding to a survey said they would use the company again, and 79% of jobs came from repeat customers—an increase of 11% over the previous year.

36
IDEA

Every Complaint Scores a Homer

Tom Dickson, owner of the Lansing Lugnuts, a Class A minor-league baseball team, based in Lansing, Mich., likes to use customer complaints as a guide for improving service. To encourage customer comments, he created a pitch: Give all 300 employees **a small notepad of complaint forms to carry at all times**, and tell them to record every complaint, no matter how small—or they'll be fired.

Now complaints (mostly small ones) come sliding home at the rate of about 50 per game. Each complaint receives a personal response, and Dickson has raw material for better customer service. Also, no one has been fired under the policy. Dickson admits the line about terminating employees for failure to record a complaint is just to get their attention. He prefers the carrot approach: his "Caughtcha doin' somethin' right" program, in which supervisors give "Lugnut Loot," worth $5 at stadium concessions, to employees seen providing good service.

Pay envelopes contain a list of complaints received, the resolutions, and the name of the employees who turned in the complaints. The biweekly feedback is critical to the success of the program, according to Dickson. "First-line staff members understand that management is listening to their observations and working to improve the workplace experience."

The Lugnuts are the first Class A team in the 125-year history of minor-league baseball to draw more than 500,000 fans in their first year of play. Dickson is convinced that the organization's customer-service focus is the reason for its success.

"My father taught me the first lesson of quality: Service to others will enrich their lives and yours. A company that can develop this focus and share it as a common value has a good chance to increase market share, associates' satisfaction, and customer loyalty. Service to others can be counted, measured, and managed. Collecting data is indeed important. But service to others must first be genuine or the data will not result in a loyal customer base."

J. WILLARD MARRIOTT JR.
chairman and president of the Marriott Corporation,
in Bethesda, Md.

37
IDEA

Revive the Routing Slip

Houston-based Pro-Mark, the world's largest manufacturer of drumsticks for musicians, drums up attention to clients' needs and positive feedback by **routing its customers' letters to targeted employees**. "Scrutinizing complaints is the only way to get better, and employees need compliments to know that customers appreciate them. Even compliments directed at someone else can spur others to provide great service," says Bari Brochstein-Ruggeri, director of sales.

Instead of posting customers' letters on the lunchroom wall or distributing copies to everyone, Pro-Mark prefers a personalized approach. When a customer's letter arrives, the names of up to one-third of the company's 30 employees are handwritten in the margin. The list functions as a routing slip to share the letter with those directly involved and others who might appreciate or learn from it. Not all letters are circulated, just those that clearly reinforce service values or suggest a need for improvement. Coworkers sign off next to their names, and some even add supportive comments.

Selective distribution has several advantages. Handwritten names make employees more likely to read and reflect on the customer's remarks. Knowing that colleagues have actually read the letter further increases the satisfaction of the complimented employee. And employees not on the list don't stop what they're doing to read something of marginal relevance to their jobs.

The individualized routing system makes employees feel included, says Brochstein-Ruggeri. "When people feel good about their jobs, they do them better. The result is better service for customers."

Nuts-and-Bolts Problem Solving

Floor employees closest to production are often best qualified to respond to customers' needs. Bob and Tom Jagemann, who run a family-owned tool-and-die shop, located in Manitowoc, Wis., **tap into the talent of their line employees by involving them in client visits**.

"Their involvement also helps raise their level of commitment to the customer," says Tom Jagemann, "because they see how the product is ultimately used and have a sense of the conditions that the customer has to deal with." Whenever a problem or defect arises, a small group of line workers is sent out with either a salesperson or an engineer to investigate. "It's better than having them sitting back here, potentially knowing the solution," Jagemann adds.

The 52-year-old company projects 1997 revenues of $30 million. Bob Jagemann attributes part of its growth to a culture that tries to avoid making a distinction between labor and management, a culture that has earned the company lifetime customers. In the past five years, Jagemann Stamping, which currently has more than 300 customers, has lost only one of the top 25 accounts that make up 95% of its business—and then, with a bit of hard work, the company managed to land the same client back.

39
IDEA

Phone Manners

Top-rate customer service often depends on doing little things right. Michael Bruns, CEO of Comtrak, a Memphis-based courier company, surveyed his customers and found that being put on hold was a top-ranked complaint. Since Bruns marketed his company as service-driven—and Comtrak handled up to 1,500 phone orders a week—he couldn't afford to ignore the problem.

By dividing the number of hours billed to his order-taking line by the number of orders taken, he estimated that customers had to wait on hold for an average of 45 seconds. Bruns decided the way to whittle down wait time to 30 seconds was to tie the phone bill to Comtrak's monthly departmental **bonus-point system**. At Comtrak, bonuses mattered to workers, adding as much as 20% to employees' paychecks. If the 30-second goal was missed, employees did not receive a bonus. If the goal was reached, employees qualified for bonuses and received extra points.

As a result, operators directed calls more carefully, dispatchers took more messages, and Comtrak hired an additional dispatcher. Bruns reported that Comtrak met its goal in seven of the first 10 months the system was in place.

Nurture the Nurturers

Do you ask employees for their opinion on improving customer service? Adept Inc., an information-technology consulting firm, headquartered in Wellesley, Mass., recommends an additional step: **ask how you can serve your employees** so they can better serve customers.

The $35-million firm surveys its consultants after one month on an assignment. The 10-minute phone interview includes questions such as "Is there anything we could do to improve upon services to you or the customers?" and "Have you been in contact with your account manager?" The researcher E-mails Adept's management and prepares a monthly report of employee responses.

"We used to wait until the end of the consultant's assignment to ask questions," says Sue Martell, marketing manager. "By adding questions on the front end, we can provide immediate support and catch problems before they get out of hand." Short-term assistance has included additional training and improvements to the employee's work space. The survey—which pulls a response rate almost three times higher than the old end-of-assignment written questionnaire—also generates ideas for improving long-term employee satisfaction.

"Consultants appreciate the support, and communications have opened up between consultants, recruiters, and account managers," says Martell. "Consultants are happier with their assignments and stay with us longer. All this translates into better service for clients."

41

IDEA

A Guarantee with Teeth

In any service business, customers appreciate the little things. But what was missing—the small, common errors—was plaguing Fringe Benefits Management, an $11-million Tallahassee, Fla., business that administers benefits plans. Faced with the loss of a major customer in 1990 because of poor service, CEO Michael Sheridan took drastic steps to save the contract.

Sheridan and his client drew up a **detailed list of performance standards, backed by cash guarantees**. For instance, Sheridan promised to maintain an average hold time of less than 40 seconds for customer-service calls—or pay a $1,000 monthly penalty. The biggest improvement has come in the number of days it takes the company to pay out claims and reimbursements. Now Fringe Benefits guarantees payment in 10 days, and lately it has averaged just three. Plus, phone hold time, which used to run up to one minute, now averages 30 seconds.

To keep mistakes to a minimum, Sheridan ties a greater part of employee compensation to guarantees. His 200 employees help set the 40-plus standards outlined in the contracts, and cash penalties are taken out of their bonus pool. Their latest guarantee promises complete customer satisfaction within 30 days. If the client is still unhappy, it can terminate the contract immediately. And Sheridan's company will even refund all fees for the 60-day period prior to contract termination.

Sheridan's guarantee makes him stand out from his much larger competitors. "We rarely are the low bidder," he says. "But clients tell us our service and our guarantees more than make up for the difference in cost."

42
IDEA

Call In the Commandos

According to an industry survey, Holy Cross Hospital, in Chicago, has climbed from the 13th to the 98th percentile in patient satisfaction rankings. How? "We declared war on poor service," says Mark Clement, president of the $98-million, 1,700-employee hospital.

Holy Cross **created a service infrastructure** of eight teams, each made up of 10 employees and leaders. To ensure overall results, a "commando team" oversees the eight teams.

1) A physician team is responsible for continuing education, new doctors' orientation, and other physician-support activities.

2) A measurement team measures and disseminates service results.

3) A linking team designs activities to reinforce service-oriented behavior: a traveling trophy for the department with the highest satisfaction scores, a luncheon honoring doers of good deeds.

4) A standards team designs measurable standards for employee behavior that affects customer satisfaction, then works to implement them.

5) A first-and-last-impression team helps employees frame the customer experience to employ the best practices.

6) A removing-irritations team acts on customer feedback.

7) A customer-satisfaction team makes sure that department-based teams develop and implement improvement initiatives.

8) An adding-value team develops amenities that exceed customer expectations, such as offering patients hair appointments.

43
IDEA

Freshly-Squeezed Customer Service

At Odwalla, a maker of fresh-fruit and nutritional juices, based in Half Moon Bay, Calif., it's the delivery-truck drivers who have face-to-face interaction with customers. The company has 175 trucks on the road, and **each driver answers questions and receives customer feedback** at every stop along the route. Odwalla has also invested millions of dollars in technology, outfitting each truck with a hand-held computer to track inventory and complete on-the-spot invoices.

Talk to the drivers and you'll find that they are the most enthusiastic advocates of the product. Odwalla goes to great lengths to educate employees about the nutritional value of its juices. It also taste-tests potential new products in-house, conducts product-naming contests among staff, and allots each employee a pint of juice for every day worked (three pints a day for drivers).

The truck drivers, says Chris Gallagher, director of communications, are Odwalla's public-relations team. And the upshot of that effort, says former-driver-turned-company-accountant Cindy Burns, is better customer service.

44
IDEA

Customer-Driven Bonus Plan

Irv Shapiro recalls summoning his managers and asking, "How many of our clients are actively referring customers to us?" Days later, the answer came back: 25%—at best.

While customers claimed to be happy with the level of service they received from Metamor, it wasn't enough for Shapiro, CEO of the $31-million computer consulting company, based in Chicago. So now he rewards employees whose customers agree to be references.

All employees qualify for a **quarterly bonus based on several performance measures**; one of which is customer feedback. After talking to customers, supervisors rate employees on a scale of one to five for each aspect of customer service. Responses from dissatisfied customers are weighted more heavily. Supervisors then meet individually with each employee to discuss the results. If a client agrees to serve as a reference and gives high marks across the board, the employee usually earns the maximum bonus for customer service.

Shapiro paid out $200,000 to his employees in customer-service bonuses. Approximately 5% of overall revenue—or as much as 13% of payroll—is set aside for the incentive program. Of that, approximately 40% goes toward incenting customer satisfaction. The result? Over a five-year period, Metamor's average contract grew 10-fold, and approximately 75% of its current accounts sang Metamor's praises to their friends—representing an increase of 50%.

45
IDEA

Weekly Praise with the Paycheck

Your service to customers is only as good as your employees. To remind them that what they do affects customers, why not **attach notes to employees' paychecks thanking them** for that week's achievement? That's the approach of Jim Johnson, president of Brandy's Automotive Repair, headquartered in Schaumburg, Ill.

Johnson personalizes his handwritten comments for each of his 70 employees. Sometimes he comments on performance, "Joe, I noticed you had a record week on number of cars served and fewest mistakes!" He might thank them, "Chris, thanks for coming in an extra half day to take care of that customer." Or, he might congratulate a mechanic on earning a bonus or having a baby. "Writing 70 comments takes time, but each employee is important, not just a number," says Johnson. "I want employees to know that I notice and appreciate their good work."

Do employees find the comments corny or paternalistic? "To the contrary," says Johnson, "they tell me they miss my notes when I'm away on vacation, and I've heard from spouses that the comments are appreciated."

Pay envelopes also include employee rankings for the Employee of the Year Contest. (The winner gets a trip to Las Vegas.) Employees are ranked on the number of customers served and error rates. The contest encourages the mechanics to be the best they can be, asserts Johnson. Linking paychecks with performance statistics and personal comments sends a message to employees that service is important because—when it comes to performance reviews and bonuses—customers impact their salaries.

Pride of Ownership

If you give people ownership of something, they take better care of it," declares Bob Ottley, owner of One Step Tree and Lawncare, in North Chili, N.Y. Acting on this belief, the company gives newly trained service representatives **a deed to their service territory**.

Although Ottley started the program in a lighthearted effort to increase employee motivation, employees have come to view receipt of the certificate as a rite of passage. He notes, "Each area representative hangs the framed deed in his or her work space with pride. The deed helps establish a sense of ownership, and employees are motivated to make their territory the best in the company."

The deed reinforces the idea that the representative has full responsibility for the territory's management, customer retention, and new sales. In the eight years since One Step began the deed program, its customer retention rate has jumped from 67% to 85%.

47
IDEA

Have I Got a Slogan for You

Corporate mission statements and slogans don't satisfy customers—people do," admits Doug Steimle, CEO of California Pools and Spas, in West Covina, Calif. Nonetheless, he believes that employees and customers value slogans as statements of corporate intentions.

Steimle uses a multimedia presentation to unveil **a new customer-oriented slogan each year** at the company banquet. One year's slogan was "Positive Performance." Another slogan proclaimed, "The Customer Is First." Steimle's favorite place to put the slogan is above the company logo on golf shirts worn by employees. "It subtly challenges our employees to live up to the visual commitment," notes Steimle. "Other people dress for success, we dress for action." In addition, he uses large print to make the slogan highly visible.

"The potential for dissatisfaction is enormous in a process that begins with heavy machinery destroying the customer's backyard," observes Steimle. "The slogan creates an invitation for a customer bothered by debris or noise to say 'Hey, what about your slogan?' It's all part of our effort to create high customer expectations and live up to them. We deliver on our promise of customer satisfaction—98% of surveyed customers say they would refer us to a friend."

48

IDEA

Favoring Family Values

Working parents constantly juggle the demands of work and family life. Employees who spend work time worrying about their children or elderly relatives spend less time working for your customers.

WFD, a 478-person provider of corporate work-life services, in Boston, knows that **helping people deal with the personal side of life**—so they can devote more energy to work—is vital to company success. WFD offers several tips on how to help employees balance work and family life.

- *Offer child-care referral services for employees.* An unforeseeable event—a sick child who can't go to day care or a babysitter who doesn't show up—adds stress to a working parent's day, and parents in this situation are often late for work. Assisting parents in emergencies can reduce stress and improve employee attendance.

- *Support parents' need for supervision of children during nonschool hours.* Some firms recruit and train child-care providers who offer programs for after-school hours or school vacations. The goal is to keep parents on the job when children have time off from school.

- *Give employees the opportunity to vary work hours*—work at home, use flextime, or compress their work week—to deal with family obligations. These variations can lead to better customer service and expanded business hours.

49
IDEA

Celebration Time

Microtest, a $50-million computer and LAN products supplier, celebrates National Customer Service Week each year. The Phoenix-based company designs a series of **activities to recognize the firm's 200 employees for their dedication to customers**. At the central event—a recognition banquet—the company presents awards based on peer nominations, customer letters, and management selection. Linda O'Keeffe, Microtest's director of channel marketing and customer operations, offers the following cautions for those considering similar events.

- *Focus on the future.* Bagel breakfasts, cookie breaks, and potluck lunches are fine, but remember that the purpose of the annual celebration is to remind people of the excellent work they have done. A week-long theme such as "Making A Difference" can reinforce this emphasis.

- *Recognize employees for service to others within the company as well as to external customers.* Everyone makes a contribution that ultimately affects the customer's experience. Don't limit your focus to employees with direct customer contact. Manufacturing, engineering, and other departments will feel slighted if they're not included.

- *Don't view the celebration as a complete recognition program.* Long-lasting motivation comes from recognizing employees "in-the-moment," not just once a year. O'Keeffe E-mailed everyone in the company to recognize one individual's effort in saving an order.

"Leaders and managers must
give guidance, not punishment, to
employees who take risks and,
occasionally, make mistakes.
Wrong decisions should be used
as the basis for training; right
decisions should be used as
the basis for praise
and positive examples."

JAN CARLZON
former CEO
of Scandinavian Airlines Systems (SAS),
in Stockholm, Sweden, and author of *Moments of Truth*
(Ballinger Publishing, 1987)

50
IDEA

All Aboard for Responsibility

"Our customers request little from our employees other than a pleasant disposition," maintains Linn Moedinger, vice-president and chief mechanical officer for the Strasburg Rail Road, a steam-powered rail service carrying 375,000 tourists and passengers a year through Pennsylvania Dutch farmland, in Lancaster County. Of course, customers also want trains to run on time, which requires a policy of zero tolerance for employee absences. Moedinger responded by designing a **scheduling system that keeps trains running and employees happy**.

Employees have to find their own replacements, in return for control over their schedules. By the 15th of each month, employees indicate the times they are available to work the following month. Moedinger juggles the requests of up to 30 full- and part-time workers and posts the schedule. After that, employees are 100% responsible for replacements. "They do switch among themselves—some months they practically erase through the paper," remarks Moedinger. "But a qualified crew member is on the job every time."

Moedinger hasn't had a scheduling problem since the company fully implemented the new system. Some workers view flexible schedules as a form of compensation for modest salaries, and contented train crews give better customer service.

Badmouthing Prohibited

To make sure employees don't clown around with the customers who fuel the growth of Sequent Computer Systems, the company depends on one of the most famous clowns of all, Bozo. More than a hundred "Bozo boxes"—receptacles to **collect fines from employees who criticize a customer or supplier**—are strategically located in conference rooms and hallways. Anyone caught by a fellow employee criticizing a customer or supplier must drop a quarter in the nearest box.

As the Beaverton, Ore., computer manufacturer grew from $4 million to $354 million during the past decade, former president Scott Gibson admits, "We had drifted a bit into the arrogance that comes from success." The Bozo boxes keep employees humble, and all proceeds go to the needy.

52

IDEA

Giving Dead-End Jobs a Future

How do you motivate entry-level employees to give excellent customer service? Carolee Pierce, general manager of Facilities Management and Consulting (FMC), a Chicago-based provider of turnkey mailroom and copy-center services with revenues of nearly $750,000, **offers employees a clear career path**.

To produce skilled, customer-centered, promotable workers, FMC does the following:

- *Broadcast upward mobility.* FMC lets employees know they'll be moving up the ladder.
- *Extensive initial training.* Workers learn every detail of a mail clerk's job, including how to address a letter properly.
- *Switchboard time.* The switchboard teaches employees how to interact well with customers. New hires practice vocal tones and making good first impressions.
- *Audiotapes and videotapes.* Videos by the U.S. Postal Service cover subjects ranging from pleasing customers to mailroom organization.
- *Users' guide.* New employees receive a simple description of what customers can expect from FMC's mail services.
- *Equipment training.* To gain experience on different types of equipment, entry-level employees rotate among two or three customer sites during their first month.
- *Constant coaching.* Managers prepare mail clerks for the next level by improving computer and communications skills.

Prescription for Burnout

All you have to do is answer customer-support phones for two hours to realize how stressful it is and how important those reps are to building customer loyalty," says Don Emery, president and CEO of $5.2-million Reference Software International, a maker of grammar-checking programs, in San Francisco. Fearful that his staff would burn out, he set aside **one day a week for customer-service reps to work on self-designed projects**.

"It went over like a raise and has benefited our company as much as it did the employees," Emery says.

One employee programmed a demonstration disk that the company would have hired an outsider to do. Another started in-house software-training classes. A third started a computer bulletin board for grammar aficionados. The quality work at bargain prices and low departmental turnover offset the cost of hiring an additional rep to cover the phone lines, reports Emery. And when they got back on the line, the reps were more likely to enjoy helping customers.

54
IDEA

Get Everyone's 2¢

Mission statements can mean a lot to the owner of a company. But how do you get line employees—working to meet deadlines, targets, and profit margins—to give more than lip service to a mission statement's promise to serve?

At Group Publishing, a religious-books publisher, based in Loveland, Colo., **employees participated in the mission-statement crafting process**. Company executives met and drafted definitions for five "core values." Employees were allowed to add their comments, which were then incorporated into the final document.

Joannie Schulz, co-owner of the company with her husband, Thom, reported that the group effort made the company's mission to serve its customers more meaningful to employees. "We also learned a few things about our own company in the process," says Schulz. "Although we had been taking care of our vendors, the purchasing department pointed out how we must meet the needs of both internal staff and our customers to be successful in the long term."

Frequent Fliers at the Keyboard

When your programmers are in such demand that they are wooed away in midproject by competing firms, how can you retain them and ensure continuity for your customers? The answer came to Dan Greenburg, president of the Allegiance Group, in Woodbury, N.Y., in the middle of the night.

At any given time, Greenburg manages up to 90 programmers who perform contract computer services for clients ranging from financial to entertainment to manufacturing. At the beginning of 1997, he began to **reward programmers with 10 frequent-flier miles for every hour they billed**. Greenburg factored in some bonus miles to enable a good programmer to earn a free domestic roundtrip within a year. Programmers have a choice of three airlines from which to choose; the only catch is that they must satisfactorily complete their projects to receive the miles.

Greenburg buys the miles for 2¢ each. So far, the cost of providing this incentive is running less than the $10,000 per year he had originally estimated. "Fewer programmers than expected have redeemed their miles," he adds, with some surprise. But, most important, his programmer-retention rate has increased, so now he and his customers are sleeping easy.

The Right Reward

Encouraging employees to become knowledgeable and achieve professional certification is sound advice for service-oriented companies. Great customer service also requires hands-on skills. At Brandy's Automotive Repair, headquartered in Schaumburg, Ill., an **incentive plan for employee certification** incorporates both elements.

Mechanics may earn $1,000 per year for each Automotive Service Excellence (A.S.E.) certification that's current—up to $9,000. The A.S.E. certification program proves that the technician is knowledgeable in a specific area of car repair. However, the bonus is awarded only if the technician's error rate is low. The full bonus is earned if, for every 200 hours of labor, the average rework rate is fewer than 0.5 cars. Thereafter, it is paid on a sliding scale: for a rework rate of .51 to .75, two-thirds of the incentive is awarded, and if the rework rate is .76 to 1.0, one-third of the incentive is paid. No bonus is paid when the rework rate is greater than 1.0.

As a result, all four Brandy shops have been accredited as A.S.E. Blue Seal of Excellence facilities, indicating a high level of technician certification. Only six other shops in Illinois have achieved the same recognition. Since the adoption of the bonus plan, the rework rate has dropped from four cars per 200 hours to only 0.37. Customers want their cars fixed properly the first time, emphasizes Johnson, and the bonus plan makes this happen.

57
IDEA

How to (T)excel at Service

Your employees are more likely to give exceptional customer service if they understand your standards of excellence. Ed Loke, for example, understands the importance of setting reasonable, specific, and measurable goals, along with rewards for achieving them. When Loke instituted his **"No Surprises Guarantee Program"** at Texcel, a Houston-based $6-million industrial rubber products wholesaler, shipping errors fell by 75%.

Loke promised that Texcel would ship goods within 24 hours, notify customers of back-ordered items prior to shipping, ship the correct goods, make no pricing errors, and provide error-free paperwork. Failing these, Texcel mails customers a "bonus" gift certificate, good for 5% off their next order. Any balance in the fund set up to cover the guarantee goes to the employees handling the orders. The result: Texcel maintains a 99.6% accuracy rate on its guarantee, and shipments have more than tripled over a 10-year period.

While the program seems to have reached a plateau in terms of shipping and invoicing mistakes, Loke believes the cumulative effect of his service focus contributes more to the bottom line than the reduced-error savings, which he estimates at more than $300,000 per year. "The value of not having to waste today's time fixing last week's mistakes is hard to calculate, but it's a huge advantage for distributors and for us," Loke says.

III

"Think about it. Right now, a whole generation of young people in the United States has been brought up to take computers for granted. Pointing with a mouse is no more mysterious to them than hitting the 'on' button on the television is to their parents."

ANDREW S. GROVE
CEO of Intel Corporation, in Santa Clara, Calif.,
and author of *Only the Paranoid Survive:
How to Exploit the Crisis Points That Challenge
Every Company and Career*
(Currency Doubleday, 1996)

IDEA

Hurry Up and Wait

How does Dr. Henry Samson, an optometrist located in New Haven, Conn., improve customer service? Samson realized that patients dread filling out "intake" forms; it takes up a great deal of time and is especially annoying when forms ask for information already provided during a prior visit.

Samson now uses an **interactive computer system to collect patient health data**. The software tailors questions to recent answers, skipping unnecessary questions. Patients can review data from their last visit to verify or modify the information. Time is saved without sacrificing personal attention.

Samson's customers are clearly pleased with the service. When given a choice of a verbal or computer interview, 95% opt for the computer.

59
IDEA

Let's Get Technical

Calling a technical support line can be a frustrating experience, especially when the customer has trouble explaining the problem. Estimation Inc., located in Linthicum Heights, Md., became the first construction-industry software supplier to encourage customers to **E-mail or fax requests for technical support and attach the actual files or folders causing the problem**. Its technical support staff can diagnose the problem quickly without the frustration of playing "20 questions" or telephone tag.

Estimation's electronic communication system results in faster and more accurate solutions. Old-fashioned phone contact required an average of three calls—sometimes as many as 10—between the customer and support staff to solve the problem. The E-mail or fax communication prior to, or simultaneous with, a phone call usually provides the proper solution with just one call.

At first, customers needed a bit of education on how to use the new electronic communications. Estimation began providing live Internet demonstrations in 1996, during its annual user group meetings, and has touted the system's benefits to customers in quarterly newsletters.

Customers who use fax and E-mail are delighted with the results, says Mary Alders, marketing supervisor of this 90-employee company. Contractors can return to their work faster, with less downtime. They also like being able to submit requests after business hours when they are finished on-site. "Those who make use of this new technology rarely call back," says Alders, "except to say thank you."

60
IDEA

Foiling Phone Frustration

Have you ever phoned your health plan to ask about a claim? Chances are, you've been transferred, put on hold, given another number to call, shunted to voice mail, or were told so-and-so would call you back. Vytra Healthcare, a 210,000-member HMO, headquartered in Melville, N.Y., responded by establishing a company goal to deal with phone frustration: Resolve every customer inquiry with one phone call.

Not too long ago, fewer than 40% of Vytra's members were able to obtain satisfaction with one phone call. Now, more than 60% need to make only one call, and 85% of those calls are answered within 30 seconds— enviable numbers for this industry. Vytra customer-service personnel make it all happen using **electronic support systems** such as comprehensive call tracking and on-screen access to member benefits information.

Member calls are dialed directly to one of five customer-service teams, each handling different customer groups. Service team members are continuously trained to handle any issue that may arise. Team members have the expertise, responsibility, and authority to handle bill adjustments, enrollments, physician selection, benefits information, claims processing, and problem resolution.

One-call-does-it-all is a big hit in member surveys, and Bill Keena, vice-president of customer service, says that "this program has measurably improved customer retention rates."

61
IDEA

Helping Your Customer's Customers

Improve your business partnerships by giving your customers the tools they need to serve their customers. Aurora Casket Company, a $90-million, 750-employee coffin manufacturer, based in Aurora, Ind., developed a **laptop computer presentation** to make it easier for funeral directors and bereaved families to plan funeral arrangements—right at home.

The self-paced computer program contains descriptions and pictures of caskets, urns, vaults, monuments, flower arrangements, clothing for the deceased, visitation options, and other funeral details. When all choices have been made, the total price for the funeral is displayed, so customers can review the itemized costs and alter selections if needed.

Aurora customizes the presentation for its larger customers—funeral directors—to show their customers the range of options available to them. "As a service to funeral directors, we include information on competitors' caskets," says Christina Kent, customer-service manager. A side benefit for Aurora is insight into what customers like about competitors' products.

The laptop presentation provides a service for both families and funeral directors. "Consumers can find it traumatic to view caskets in a funeral home," says Kent, "so a computer selection process in the consumer's home is a more appealing option. The more consumers are informed about their choices, the better they feel about their decisions."

Aurora and its funeral directors are pleased with the results. Unit sales at funeral homes that make full use of the software have increased 10%. "Helping customers build their businesses is a good way to build our own," says Kent.

62
IDEA

A Fertile Field for Voice Mail

Voice mail is an efficient way to communicate with employees. Margaret Cook, executive director of the Assisted Reproductive Technology Program, thought it would work with customers, too. The Birmingham, Ala., fertility clinic expanded its voice-mail system to **give up to 10,000 clients individual voice-mail boxes**.

Patients can dial an 800 number to retrieve messages at their convenience, day or night. A confidential PIN ensures security. "We need to be in constant communication with our customers about the timing of appointments and the results of routine procedures," says Cook. Even if all clients had message machines at home or work, Cook wouldn't want to leave confidential messages others might hear, and the alternative—telephone tag—is an inconvenience for both customers and staff.

The phone system also allows patients to retrieve prerecorded instructions and answers to frequently asked questions. Patients can use another 800 number to leave questions for a nurse, who supplies the answer with a phone call or by leaving a message in the patient's voice-mail box.

Feedback from customers has been positive, says Cook. Staff have learned to leave complete messages that don't confuse patients; they also have developed a sense of what information is too sensitive for a recorded message. "Now that the staff is experienced with the system, complaints are minimal," says Cook, "which says a lot in our emotionally intense business. The voice-mail system makes us responsive to customers by providing an effective, confidential way to relay information."

63

IDEA

Webmeister Magic

When Cathey Cotten, owner of MetaSearch, a technical recruiting company located in San Anselmo, Calif., shared information about potential job candidates with clients, she didn't bother with faxes or letters. Instead, Cotten posted résumés at **password-protected customer pages** on MetaSearch's Web site. "The turnaround time is great," said Cotten. "If you fax a résumé, it literally sits there for days or gets lost." Cotten's system alerted her when a client read a résumé, reminding her to follow up with a phone call.

Doug Wright, president of $2-million Wright Communications, also has password-protected Web pages. The New York City graphic-design company's site enables clients to view work in progress, approve changes, or sign off on finished work by E-mail. Wright can set up a new client page in less than a half hour. Before he makes a sales call, he prepares a page for the prospective customer. "It makes us look like one of the big guys," Wright notes.

64
IDEA

Together at Last

Automation should improve customer service. At least that's what Andras Hites, president of Micro Dental Laboratories, in Dublin, Calif., thought. So Hites wasn't happy when he realized that his $23.5-million company was still wasting customers' time. For example, dentists would often return calls to the laboratory without knowing the name of the lab technician who had originally tried to reach them, launching what often became a lengthy search to find the right technician.

In response, Hites decided to install a computer network, bought state-of-the-art phones, and **linked the phone system to the network** with software from AnswerSoft, called Sixth Sense with SoftPhone. The total system cost amounted to approximately $35,000.

Today, when a lab technician contacts a customer, he or she calls up the customer's file and clicks on the "dial" command. If the customer isn't in, the technician notes the attempt in an electronic phone log that's stored in the customer's file. The software can also schedule calls, and it allows voice and fax functions to be used simultaneously. Another benefit: Sixth Sense allows Hites to monitor how many times a customer has been in contact with the lab.

Online Tête-à-Tête

One way to cut down on mounds of wasted paper and expensive overnight courier bills is to create a Web site. But what if your customers aren't Web users? An alternative is a **private online system** that can give your customers access to price lists, product literature, sales representatives, even the Internet. All they need is a computer, a modem, and your system's phone number.

Hinrichs Financial Group, in Charlotte, N.C., established its own online system in 1996. Hinrichs is using its system as a pipeline to its own agents, who download the documents, spreadsheet files, and graphics they need to build custom proposals. Product information and the firm's weekly newsletter are available on the system. A built-in security feature limits the files that agents can open.

There are distinct advantages to having your own online system. On the Web you're just another face in the crowd. But with your own system, you'll gain visibility. It's the primary destination for your customers rather than a stopover on the way to other sites. And if you make that system a real source of service—a place where your customers can get information and let you know what they need—you'll be strengthening your relationship with them.

"Consumers are statistics.
Customers are people."

STANLEY MARCUS
Chairman Emeritus,
Neiman Marcus, in Dallas

To Eliminate Frustration, Press "1"

With some of the new automatic-call-distributor (ACD) technology available today, the telephone can be the best way to produce great customer service—or the worst. How can you determine whether your customer-service procedures are user-friendly? One option is to call your own customer-service line. By posing as a customer, you'll be able to figure out if the ACD menu is too complex or if your customers are kept waiting for too long.

To ensure that senior managers understand your standards, make them **experience customer service at the lowest acceptable point**. If you allow customers to wait on hold for 10 minutes, let your managers experience a 10-minute hold. A standard may look good on paper, but when translated into reality, it should push employees to tighten standards. Also, give managers the opportunity to take customer-service calls.

Two simple tricks can turn problems with ACDs into benefits: Have the system tell customers how long they're going to have to wait. And let customers choose a priority for the call. This option can eliminate the feeling of helplessness that often overwhelms callers when they hear automated instructions.

67
IDEA

Accurate and Instantaneous Info—Anywhere!

Computerized databases give on-site or remote technicians the information they need to respond to customers' problems. One of their best features is the contact record—a computer record that stores information about a customer's interaction with the company. The customer doesn't have to waste time repeating the problem to one service technician after another.

When you create your system, make it flexible. It should have the ability to override data-entry fields and include a comment field for entering customer or rep instructions, questions, problems, and complaints. You'll also need to ensure that your base-level inventory is accurate and that your database stays in sync with it. Haven't we all called a company to ask if it has a certain product, been told that the product is in stock, and then driven across town to purchase it—only to find that what the computer reported was wrong?

To test how well your computerized databases meet your customers' needs, pretend to be a customer. See how flexible your systems are under nonstandard conditions, and check the accuracy of your online inventory.

68
IDEA

Call Us on the Computer

E-mail has opened up new avenues of customer service. Here are a few ways in which companies are **using online communication**:

- Checkfree Corp., an electronic-payment company, located in Columbus, Ohio, trains its customer-service reps in both phone and E-mail etiquette—and with good reason. Two-thirds of the department's calls arrive by E-mail. Without having to log on to a commercial service, customers can ask why a check was posted a day early and receive a reply within 24 hours.

- A Cincinnati package-design firm was nudged into the digital age by a major client. When Procter & Gamble requested a quick turn-around on uncontracted work from Libby Perszyk Kathman, account executive Nancy Gooch E-mailed her proposed budget, and within 24 hours the client approved it.

- A commercial printer located in Spokane, Wash., receives some customers' instructions by E-mail. Chris Snider, sales manager at United Lithographers, explains, "We insert the price and the purchase-order number and send it back with the customer's instructions as confirmation."

- Joe Boxer uses the Internet to reach its younger fans. The San Francisco clothing company promotes its E-mail address on clothing hangtags and on billboards. Customer feedback is plentiful as a result.

69
IDEA

Lost and Found

Does this sound familiar? A busy CEO installs an automated phone-answering system, figuring it will save lots of time and money. "At first clients said it was terrific," recalls Ed Winguth, owner of a $1-million executive-search firm, in Los Altos, Calif. But soon customers started saying the system was too cold and annoying because it forced callers to sit through three levels of menus before reaching a human voice. Repeat customers really got annoyed.

Winguth, Donahue & Co. finally **scrapped the system** after two years, suffering $4,000 in repairs and six days of downtime—and the loss of four prospective clients. What's more, Winguth realized a larger truth from his experience: If clients could complain so heartily about the phones, what else was on their minds?

Winguth realized he also needed to follow up with repeat clients after making a placement. His new approach proves that a lost customer is an ideal prospect. And Winguth recently won back a client after five years.

Online Is on Target

At Balentine & Co., a midsize investment firm, based in Atlanta, the ability to **comb the Internet for hard data and quick feedback** allows consultants to bolster their investment advice with up-to-the-minute detail. These days you'll find Balentine's consultants routinely trolling Web sites, mail lists, and newsgroups to help customers who are contemplating market investments or are in need of feedback on product innovations.

Gary Martin, a Balentine consultant, discovered that the Internet can be a dynamic business resource—but the discovery was something of a shot in the dark. Following a lunchtime chat with a client who wished to develop a design for a plastic wheelchair but wasn't sure how to gauge market interest, Martin offered to browse the Net for the client. Using a few keywords, he quickly found a newsgroup for people with handicaps and posted a message asking users for feedback on the idea. Within a few weeks, Martin had heard back from enough users to be able to pass along encouraging news to his client: Most respondents had found the prospect of lightweight wheelchairs very appealing.

71
IDEA

Getting Smart Online

While cruising the Internet one day, former Invitrogen Corp. research scientist David Higgins happened on a newsgroup for reagents in which a user was trouncing one of Invitrogen's products. Higgins quickly fired off a response, identifying himself as an employee, and offered tips on better use of the product.

Higgins' move was a natural first step, in fact, for companies wanting to establish an online presence. Out of the Internet's thousands of newsgroups and mailing lists, a significant number are devoted to discussions of specific industries, products, or services. With customers, suppliers, and competitors mixing it up online, there are plenty of opportunities for controlling damage, providing service and support, and collecting feedback.

Now Invitrogen employees regularly cruise the Internet as part of the company's customer-service routine. The $28-million manufacturer of gene expression kits and reagents, based in Carlsbad, Calif., hired a Webmaster **to scan relevant Usenet groups for messages about the company and its products**. The rest of the time he answers technical-help questions from baffled customers—many from overseas—via E-mail.

The Internet's unbounded flow of ideas and opinions has intensified Invitrogen's commitment to customer service. Word travels fast in cyberspace, making it all the more important for companies to get their own presence out there.

Jump In Together

Ventana Medical Systems, a biomedical instrument and reagent manufacturer, in Tucson, maintains an online customer database that alerts service reps to a customer's history and current issue resolution status.

The database program saves valuable time for Ventana and its customers. It also sends a message to customers that the company is actively working to solve their problems. "We get lots of good feedback on our efficiency in resolving problems," says Mary Bradley, customer-service supervisor.

Problems in the biomedical-manufacturing industry tend to be complex ones requiring an extended resolution period. Some of Ventana's 1,000 customers like to participate in the search for a solution, while others prefer to wait until the company generates one. Ventana uses the database to code each customer's problem by subject. Those who wish to participate in the solution can be put in touch with each other to form a **problem-resolution network**. When a solution is found, the customers who were waiting for it can be contacted quickly.

Bon Appetit!

When restaurant customers are conversing during a meal, they don't want interruptions from an intrusive public-address system. According to Steve Damian, assistant general manager of the Border Cafe, in Cambridge, Mass., loud announcements whenever a table is ready disturb diners already seated. Because the bar area can get very noisy, waiting customers worry that they will miss their page. The solution: **Give customers a personal beeper to signal when their tables are ready**.

The 115-employee Tex-Mex restaurant began using the beeper system in 1991. The average wait on a busy night is about one hour. Customers can sit in the lounge and engage in conversation, or, weather permitting, stroll outside the restaurant. "We serve 2,000 customers on a busy day." says Damian. "Both waiting and dining customers really enjoy not having to listen to constant overhead paging."

74
IDEA

Loan Ranger

Monday through Friday, nine to five, may not be convenient hours for your customers. This was clearly the case at Granite State Credit Union, in Manchester, N.H., where the majority of auto-loan customers shopped for cars during the evening, after the office was closed. Customers were forced to wait until the next day to get information on rates and book values, or to apply for a loan.

To address the situation, Granite State **extended its lending hours by giving a cellular phone to one loan officer each evening**. Customers can call the extended-hours lending line until 11 p.m. to obtain information or submit an application. "Customers love the fact that they can get the loan services they want, when they need them," says Michele Duhamel, Granite State's compliance manager. Applications received during the evening are reviewed first thing the next morning.

Convenient access to services is important to customers. Duhamel notes that ATMs have made most banking services available when customers need them, but auto-loan services haven't been as accessible. Extending lending hours via the phone is Granite State's way of matching hours of operation with customer needs.

Efficiency in Any Language

Customize your database, integrate it into every aspect of your business, and keep it current, advises Irene Agnew, president of Agnew Tech-II, a Westlake Village, Calif., communication firm that specializes in foreign language translation. The firm customized a program called Approach to create its client database. Here's how the technology works for Agnew Tech-II:

- *Fast service.* The system's quotation module converts the number of words to be translated into production work-hour requirements and costs. Customers with rush orders can receive a written quotation within 10 minutes of requesting a bid via the Internet.

- *Quick assessment of freelance staff availability.* The program identifies which of Agnew's 300 freelance translators have the skills for the assignment.

- *Inter-department communications.* When a project is approved, the system sends a complete work order to the production department. The computer automatically prints the daily status of work orders and can send reports to clients, if necessary. When a job is finished, the accounting department prints the invoice. The number of hours worked is recorded to monitor the accuracy of bids and detect changes needed in the quotation formula.

- *Client data.* The database provides a comprehensive history of each client at the click of a button. "When customers ask us questions about prior work months later," says Agnew, "we can easily comply."

Customers compliment Agnew Tech-II on its rapid response and efficient job monitoring. And happy clients provide word-of-mouth referrals for the firm.

Blockbuster Videos

Taking minutes at client meetings helps everyone remember decisions and details, but the process can disrupt the meeting. The scribe is too busy writing to participate fully in the discussion, and the free flow of ideas may be interrupted by catch-up questions. To make meetings doubly useful for customers, Edgewater Technology began **videotaping design conferences on long-term projects as an alternative to note taking**. "The tapes construct accurate minutes and much more," says Shirley Singleton, CEO of the $12-million software solutions developer, in Wakefield, Mass.

New hires on both the client and supplier sides can be brought up to speed on a project quickly. Videos give them a chance to see what went into the decisions—why a technology was chosen, or what ideas were rejected. Original participants can refresh their memories as well.

Sometimes Singleton constructs a video collage from the tapes to show at the celebration following the project's completion. "Clients get a kick out of seeing how far the project has come," Singleton says. "They also use the clips for their own multimedia presentations. We take the role of a personal coach with our clients, teaching them how to jazz up their presentations so they look stronger to their own management."

77
IDEA

Log On Before Check-In

Customer satisfaction can soar if you help customers with their planning. Hospitality Partners, a management company responsible for 10 hotels in the Washington, D.C., area, makes trip planning easier for their guests with **online advice and information**. In 1996, the company partnered with America Online's Digital Cities program, which provides details on tourist attractions, tours, restaurants, and accommodations. The program includes an E-mail address for the "Tacky Tourist," a hotel employee who answers questions about the city. The "Tacky Tourist" also answers questions live in a chat room for three hours each evening. Hotel guests are told about the service when reservation confirmations are sent.

"Customers love the 'Tacky Tourist'," says Holly Boginis, corporate director of marketing. "About 30 people visit the site every day. It helps them prepare for their visits and have better trips. By interacting with the 'Tacky Tourist,' visitors feel as if they have a friend in Washington before they get here. Many say the site saved them a lot of time."

The online tourist information service is more than just an added expense for the $80-million hotel group, which hosts 375,000 guests per year. According to Boginis, the online program brought in $200,000 in revenues last year.

Fully Wired

A.G. Findings and Manufacturing, a manufacturer of beeper accessories, in Sunrise, Fla., is adept at **using technology to enhance customer service**. A.G.'s director of marketing, Elena Van Scoyoc, recommends the following tech-tips that helped her company stay on top of customer needs:

- Use fully equipped PCs instead of "dumb" terminals for every employee. (Dumb terminals rely on a mainframe computer for all processing, applications, data retrieval, and storage; they cannot operate without being connected to the mainframe.) Employees need access to information, such as product inventory levels, to serve customers. When an issue involves other departments, service reps can use E-mail or text message screens to relay details on the customer's situation. This can be done at the same time a customer is being transferred by phone.
- Use online schedulers or calendars to remind employees of important dates and meetings, plan follow-up phone calls, and organize timetables for providing services to customers.
- Update information systems daily, and at the end of the day, call every customer who placed an order that day to confirm their shipments and costs. Take advantage of this call to ask if the customer needs anything else.
- Get a phone system that pages managers when they have a message on their voice mail so that they can respond immediately to customers with urgent needs.

"Full use of technology has helped us become a leader in our market," Van Scoyoc states. "We could do the job with lesser technologies, but we wouldn't be as fast or as customer conscious."

79
IDEA

Constant Comment

Are you tired of tracking customer complaints with inefficient paper systems? So was AFFINA Corp., a Troy, Mich., supplier of market-research and database-management services. The company uses customer feedback to improve its operations, and it conveys the feedback to 25 other companies that outsource call-center activities to AFFINA.

Its solution was a **feedback database accessible to every employee** at the click of a mouse. The computerized system makes it possible for AFFINA to categorize and track large numbers of comments, as well as track the status of complaint resolution. To provide insight into customer feelings, positive and neutral comments—even small ones—are collected, along with complaints.

Employees are encouraged to enter their comments into the system. "Approximately 25% of entries into the system are employee comments rather than direct customer comments," says account executive Margaret Raddatz. "Both types of comments have led to operational improvements, so it would be a mistake to limit the database to customer comments."

The database tracks the number and types of comments as well as complaint resolution time. One of the system's best features, according to Raddatz, is the ability to rapidly identify trends in comments entered by 200 different call-center representatives. For example, one client initiated a 700,000-piece direct mail solicitation with a flawed mailing list. Within the first two days of inbound calls, AFFINA noticed that many recipients weren't eligible for the offer. The client was able to remove 125,000 ineligible names before the mailing was completed. The client saved postage and avoided untold customer dissatisfaction.

Give Them Credit for Complaining

Smart companies purge duplicate names and addresses from their mailing lists, but duplicates can slip through even the most sophisticated systems. J. Jill, a Meredith, N.H., mail-order company that sells natural-fiber clothing for women, tries to save customers the inconvenience of having to deal with such unwanted mail. "Our catalog is printed on recycled paper, but an unwanted catalog is still a waste of resources, recycled or not," notes Liesel Walsh, manager of database marketing. J. Jill offers **a $5 credit coupon to customers who alert the company to a duplicate mailing**.

Why bother? "By using the precise mailing-label information from duplicate catalogs, we can improve the computer logic used to clean our mailing lists," says Walsh. Printing and mailing costs add up quickly. Eliminating just one duplicate mailing saves about $20 a year. Customers appreciate it too: Some are concerned about the environment, and some simply find it a nuisance to deal with piles of heavy catalogs. By alerting the company to duplicates, everyone makes a positive step toward a cleaner environment.

"Your database will be a valuable
resource only if you commit
to the development of data and
research. It is better to wait
a year to start the process than
to implement a plan
that is destined to fail because
it lacks the foundation
necessary for success."

ROB JACKSON
executive vice-president and general manager
of CMS Inc., in Chapel Hill, N.C.,
and coauthor of *Strategic Database Marketing*
(NTC Business Books, 1994)

81
IDEA

Leave No Stone Unturned

Customers with complaints become apostles for the competition. When CEO and chairman Jim Thompson realized this truth in 1990, he challenged employees at his company, Electronic Controls Co. (ECCO), a Boise, Idaho, manufacturer of warning lights and backup alarms for commercial vehicles, to stamp out complaints.

Concerned that underlying problems that had provoked complaints might prompt future gripes, the customer-service team devised a form to **record detailed information about each complaint** and ECCO's corrective action. A sales-team secretary entered each complaint into a database, broken down into primary- and secondary-root causes. The most common cause, order entry, was further broken down into three areas: duplicate purchase-order number, incorrect address, and incorrect freight method. This new procedure reduced the occurrences of these three errors by 43% over a one-year period.

Once corrective action had been taken, the team leader filed the original hard copy of each resolved case in a binder entitled "closed." Complaints that merited further consideration were placed in the "open" binder. ECCO used the database to generate a monthly customer-satisfaction report that listed complaints by category and frequency of occurrence.

Ed Zimmer, ECCO's president and chief operating officer, says that this system minimized chronic problems. "In a recent 12-month period, we had 33 complaints about shipments that were either over or under the right quantity," Zimmer says. "In the first six months since we redesigned our packing slips and added a second check of each box before it was sealed, we only had six such complaints."

Computing for the Customer

When you **put technology into the hands of your salespeople**, you empower them to deliver up-to-the-minute service on the spot. A case in point is Eric Hepner, a salesman for Leegin Creative Leather Products, a belt manufacturer located in Industry, Calif.

Among Hepner's customers is a trendy men's clothing store called L.A. Sporting Club, in West Hollywood. First, Hepner takes inventory of Sporting Club's belt racks. He accesses the L.A. Sporting Club account on his laptop computer and records the count for each style number. Soon the computer's printer is spewing out reports: L.A. Sporting Club's orders in the past 12 months, compared with last season's and last year's number of belts sold—by individual style, category, color, nearly anything that Hepner and L.A. Sporting Club co-owner Don Zuidema might want to see. Then Hepner shows Zuidema some new styles that fit well with the Club's top sellers, and a few others that his laptop indicates are selling well in similar stores.

The information provided by Hepner's computer has changed the nature of the vendor-customer relationship. According to Zuidema, the objectivity of the numbers engenders trust, and he can maximize sales in what was traditionally a forgotten corner of the store. The result of Leegin's high-tech customer service? More business for both company and customer.

Virtual Roundtable

Janice Gjertsen, director of business development for Digital City New York, an online entertainment company, in New York City, believes strongly in testing new programs. But when she wanted to gauge reaction to her company's Web site, an events guide to the city, she added a twist to the traditional roundtable by **taking her focus group online**. It proved to be more effective and a lot less expensive.

To facilitate the focus-group idea, Gjertsen contacted Cyber Dialogue, also located in New York City, which is a company that specializes in online database marketing and online market research. Cyber Dialogue drew from its database of some 12,000 people for the focus group, provided the moderator, and superimposed the focus group in a chat room on Digital City's "Total New York" Web site. Gjertsen looked on from her desktop computer and used software that let her interact with the moderator without the focus group knowing.

Priced at $3,000, Cyber Dialogue's online focus group cost one-third that of a traditional group. And the results were immediate: instead of the usual four weeks, Gjertsen received a full report in a day.

The results surprised Gjertsen: "People were more honest online than they were in our traditional groups," she says.

84
IDEA

Fax for Flounder, Call for Cod

Fast turnaround time on orders is a sure way to satisfy customers and increase business. For Tasos Argiras, president of Sparta Fish, based in Manchester, N.H., two purchases of office equipment and one directive solved a nagging problem at his company.

Each day at dawn, Argiras buys some 2,000 pounds of fish and shellfish on the docks of the nearby Atlantic, then he and his three coworkers cut and package it for delivery to restaurants. But figuring out which fish to buy proved difficult, because restaurant owners didn't place orders until late morning, long after Argiras had gone to the docks. Back at his office, Argiras always found himself short on time for processing orders and unable to plan purchases in advance.

So, he installed an answering machine and a fax machine in his office and **asked customers to place their orders at night**, when they were closing their restaurants and had a good sense of their needs for the next day. Now Argiras heads for the docks knowing what kind and quantity of fish to buy. The machines also allow fishermen to leave word of the day's specials before the boats even reach shore. "We are known for our fast service," says Argiras. "The machines have made us even faster and more accurate. The restaurant owners like that. The machines have increased our business by at least 5% to 10%."

85
IDEA

Taming the Data Beast

Using a marketing database to help you anticipate customers' needs can enhance customer service. But how can you **keep your database under control**? Some tips from the experts:

- *Be choosy about the information you track.* Says Lon Orenstein, president of Computer Support Network, in Dallas, "When I ask people what they want to track about customers, I get answers like what color boxer shorts someone likes—details that don't pay off—and maintenance is a bear."

- *Develop a simple rating system.* You must be able to tell at a glance how important each customer is to your company. Bob Dorf of Marketing 1:1, in Stamford, Conn., suggests assigning each customer a score on several variables, such as past sales, potential sales, and referrals.

- *Keep your list clean.* Give thought to how names should be entered, so that a customer like IBM isn't also entered as International Business Machines.

- *Identify the best leads*—and then turn them over as quickly as possible. Put questionable prospects into a "holding" database and dead leads into a purge file, advises database specialist Linda Keating of JL Technical Group, in Palo Alto, Calif.

- *Be realistic.* If you can't get people to enter information in your database regularly, the database won't be of much use. Dorf recalls one company that devised this solution: Computer-shy executives relay information about customers to a voice-mail box; an assistant enters the messages in the database.

Discretion Is the Better Part of Value

Companies that aren't careful about how they collect and use customer information risk doing more harm than good. There's a fine line between aggressive one-to-one relationship marketing and invasion of privacy, says Stephen M. Silverman, owner of a men's apparel chain in North Dakota.

You can find your customers' addresses through their credit-card numbers. And you do need addresses to send out customized mailings. But it's not worth the risk of angering customers. You can ask customers for their address when you write up a purchase, but doing so may trigger fears of ending up on multiple mailing lists.

Credit-card siphoning isn't the only way to offend customers' sense of privacy. Imagine telling a salesperson that you're looking for a gift for someone you're dating, unaware that the details will be typed into a database. Long after the relationship has soured, you stop by the store—only to be greeted by an unfamiliar salesperson making suggestions for romantic gifts. Some customers are put off by a store's tracking of even basic information, such as birthdays or clothing sizes.

So what's a retailer to do? What's called for is **sensitivity to customers who are offended by information gathering** and careful records in your database noting their preferences. It also helps to train salespeople to put customers at ease before asking for an address—and to back off if a customer shows any reticence.

"Technology is only an enabler.
We don't need to go faster;
we need to develop a deeper
relationship with each
of our customers."

ERNAN ROMAN
president of
Ernan Roman Direct Marketing Corp.
in Douglas Manor, N.Y.,
and author of *Integrated Direct Marketing:*
The Cutting Edge Strategy for Synchronizing Advertising,
Direct Mail, Telemarketing and Field Sales
(NTC Business Books, 1995)

Minding Manners Online

Paul Richardson, founder of Russian Information Services (RIS), a publisher and distributor of books about traveling, based in Montpelier, Vt., uses the Internet to keep his customers informed and to prospect for new ones. **Courtesy is the basis of his online service policy**. Here are his dos and don'ts for selling in cyberspace.

- *Check in frequently.* Don't let messages go unanswered for more than 48 hours. If a week elapses without a reply, the person who posted the message will think nobody can help.

- *Put up the right billboard.* Because some people search postings using keywords, keep the subject fairly general. "Russia Travel" ensures that interested users find RIS's postings.

- *Look for the right lead.* Respond only if you have something to add.

- *Let others eavesdrop.* Post your responses to the whole forum. RIS gets responses all the time from people who see a message posted to someone else.

- *Keep it brief.* The medium dictates being direct and to the point. Before you start posting, listen in for a few weeks to get the tone of the forum.

- *Tailor the pitch.* Keep messages personal and address needs directly. Someone else who reads the message may think, "Hey, if they have information on that, maybe they have information on what I'm interested in."

- *Drop a business card.* Include a "signature file": a standard message at the end of your posting that tells who you are, along with a low-key description of what you do. Putting "We're your #1 supplier!" at the end of your E-mail would be too aggressive for this medium.

88 IDEA

Accurate Interpretation

Marketing to another country presents challenges beyond the language barrier, as William Hunt discovered firsthand. Hunt struck out when he tried to market his earthquake kit in Japan's largest department stores. So his wife, a native of Hiroshima, helped him develop a Web page in Japanese. Now Hunt has a new business: helping small companies market their products and services via the World Wide Web to Japan, in Japanese.

Hunt's company, Global Strategies Inc., in Alhambra, Calif., helps clients **understand their customers' culture** to avoid the mistakes entrepreneurs often make when they try to sell to the Japanese (or other overseas clients).

- Forget about scoring big with an English-only Web page. Listings on Japanese-only Web search engines are critical.
- The Japanese are often leery of overseas companies, so stating a return policy can ease their worries.
- Hunt's translators alert companies whenever their logos or themes are likely to strike a sour chord with Japanese consumers.
- Japanese audiences respond positively to the use of symbols or characters on Web pages. Hunt is likely to suggest that his clients find a mascot.

Hunt assesses potential clients' products to decide if they have much chance of selling under any conditions. If your product won't fly with Japanese males in their 20s and 30s, he says, there probably isn't much the Web can do for you. The hottest Web-marketed products in Japan: outdoor sporting goods, software and hardware, popular-music CDs, gourmet-cooking items, and clothing.

89
IDEA

Swat Those Bugs

Jeffrey Bezos, founder of the online bookstore Amazon.com, **tested his giant World Wide Web site before opening it up** to the Web at large. Employees gave friends the site's address and a fake credit-card number and asked them to place mock orders.

The planned six-week test period mushroomed into three months, as the 300 users reported bug after bug. "It was a huge success," Bezos reports. "We found all the major and most minor bugs." He now recommends a trial run to even the smallest sites. "Most people just put a site up and learn about the bugs over time. But the problem with that is the first people who try it may just give up and never come back," he notes.

Client Information at a Glance

Keeping multiple schedules and various large-scale events running smoothly can be a monumental task—but in the events management industry, absolute timeliness can make or break a company. Rita Bloom, owner of Creative Parties, based in Bethesda, Md., now runs her entire business using groupware. She keeps her $3-million company on track by relying on Lotus Notes—a software tool for which she paid a hefty $45,000.

This software helps her operation **keep close tabs on clients**. From their workstations, staff members can retrieve information, in just about any form, relating to every phase of the event-planning process. When Bloom calls up a client's name, she immediately has access to relevant correspondence, floor plans, schedules of events, invoices, and even scanned-in photos of musicians and fabric swatches.

If a client wants to add, say, the name of a new master of ceremonies, Bloom quickly calls up a new vendor sheet and fills in all the required information. When a client or supplier calls with an urgent question, in just seconds an employee can supply the answer. Recently, for example, a caterer called with a desperate last-minute query: Should the tablecloths be pure white or yellow and white? Bloom simply called up the event on screen, scrolled down, and found a picture of the fabric swatch for guests' tables. She was able to redirect the caterer to the better choice.

Bloom's software-based management enables her to please customers and expand business. "We don't look like a small-town mom-and-pop operation anymore," she says. "We look like a 21st-century company."

"It is easy to go off track
with technology, wasting money
and turning off service providers
and customers alike."

LEONARD L. BERRY
professor of marketing,
Texas A&M University, and author of
On Great Service: A Framework for Action
(The Free Press, 1995)

Fax Free-for-All

Like many companies, Central States Manufacturing installed a toll-free number to make it more attractive for customers to contact the Lowell, Ark., manufacturer of metal building components. Customers would use the toll-free number to call in their orders for rolled-form metal panels, which are used in the construction of commercial and industrial buildings. But, because a typical order consists of 15 to 25 line items, mistakes or misunderstandings commonly occurred on either end of the phone. So, Rick Carpenter, president of Central States Manufacturing, installed a fax machine to reduce order errors and to save time for both his sales reps and his customers.

But a funny thing happened once he installed the fax line: Very few customers used it. When he asked why, nearly all of them said they would rather avoid the cost of a long-distance fax and use the toll-free phone number instead. Central States responded by installing its **toll-free fax line** in 1991. Six years later, that line handles approximately 25% of the company's orders. Carpenter estimates that the toll-free fax costs his $31-million company less than $120 per month. "It's a simple thing," he says, "but it really works."

Chime for Immediate Attention

Fred McKenna, president of Orion Systems Group, in Ronkonkoma, N.Y.—a developer of administrative software for agencies catering to the disabled—was proud that every phone call was answered within three rings. However, as the business grew, picking up the phone quickly became increasingly difficult and stressful. McKenna resisted hiring a receptionist—he didn't want to dedicate the overhead and wasn't sure how to ensure quality in that position. Later, when he installed a sophisticated, expensive voice-mail system for his company, customers became frustrated when they got voice mail without the option of speaking to an operator.

Finally, Orion's voice-mail system supplier came up with a $300 solution: Two **electronic chimes**, not too dissimilar from doorbells, were mounted on the walls of the office within earshot of all 24 employees. Callers wishing to speak to someone immediately are now directed to press a certain number in the voice-mail system, which in turn rings the chimes throughout the office. "The chimes let anyone, anywhere know that someone is trying to reach one of us immediately, and a special button on all of our phones allows any of us to pick up and field the call," says McKenna. "Now I'm confident that anyone who picks up the phone will provide good service."

IV

"Never forget what business you
and your company really
are in: the business of
customer acquisition and care.
Put someone in charge of
identifying, locating, and bringing
in the best new customers, and
someone else in charge of loving
the customers you already have..."

STAN RAPP AND THOMAS L. COLLINS
cofounders of Rapp Collins Worldwide, N.Y.,
and coauthors of *The New Maximarketing*
(McGraw-Hill, 1996)

Great Expectations

Firms with a "satisfaction guaranteed" policy know that unrealistic expectations, rather than faulty products or service, often cause customer dissatisfaction. The solution is to **educate customers about what they should expect**.

🙠 Robyn Miller, the general manager for eight Fantastic Sam's hair salons, in Louisville, Ky., scrutinizes customer complaints as a guide to creating customer education cards. One card, which explained how to care for a permanent, noted the importance of returning to the salon for a follow-up trim. More customers began returning for trims, and the number of dissatisfied customers asking to have the perm redone dropped by 25%. The perms were the same. Better customer education made the difference.

🙠 Dr. Henry Samson, a New Haven, Conn., optometrist, has had fewer complaints since he began giving patients an individualized computer printout listing the activities for which each pair of glasses will and will not be ideal. Samson finds that patients who understand that different prescriptions are needed for different activities, such as close-up handicrafts, watching television, and golfing in bright sunshine, are more satisfied with their glasses. Patients who want better vision now buy several pairs of glasses—and everyone benefits. Customer education also helps patients who don't want to or can't afford to buy more than one pair of glasses. Those who understand the trade-offs of a single prescription—and choose to accept them—are more satisfied with their glasses.

Know the M.O.

Cold calls are incredibly intrusive because they aren't sensitive to your customer's schedule," says Dave Rogers, president of Information Control System (ICS). To make sure his Charlotte, N.C., data-processing consulting firm shows total respect for the client, he maintains a **database that includes communication preferences** for each client.

ICS contacts customers only when and how each prefers to be contacted. At the end of the first sales call, prospective clients are asked what forms of communication are convenient, including options such as lunch meetings or E-mail. Secretaries are also a good source of information. Some contacts aren't choosy, but knowing which ones are is important. And this sensitivity continues long after the firm lands the account.

"Each client's personality is unique," notes Rogers. "Some like breakfast meetings, some prefer an end-of-the-day drink, some need daily reassurance, and some just want us to do our work without bothering them. By keeping close tabs on the time, form, and frequency of communication that works for the customer, we understand how the client operates. The end result is that we add value to the relationship because we don't aggravate the buyer."

Diplomacy for Debts

It's easier to collect money from a satisfied customer than to wring cash from someone with whom you've severed ties. It's essential to **write collection letters with an eye toward preserving customer relationships**. Les Kirschbaum, president of Mid-Continent Agencies, a collection agency, in Rolling Meadows, Ill., offers these tips:

- *Avoid threats.* This advice makes good business sense when an account has only recently become overdue. "If you warn a customer whose account is 45 days overdue that the quality of your service will suffer, you're putting people in a situation where they have nothing to lose," says Kirschbaum.

- *Write clearly and concisely.* "Don't bury your message in all kinds of wordy sentences," says Kirschbaum. To ensure that the basic message comes across clearly, he suggests showing a draft to someone outside your industry and asking if it's easily understood.

- *Take prompt action.* "If you don't bill your customers until a couple of months after they receive your service, there's no reason for them to take your bill seriously, because you don't," Kirschbaum advises. Send an invoice promptly, follow up with a friendly collection letter at 30 days, and telephone overdue accounts 10 to 14 days later. If there's still no response, send a more serious letter within a week. Bring in a collection agency or lawyer when receivables are 90 to 120 days old.

Education, Enthusiasm, and Experience

As the U.S. leader in kayak manufacturing, Perception Inc., based in Easley, S.C., has done more than just stay afloat during its 20 years in business. In 1995, Perception realized that although it had a prime dealer network and the broadest distribution in the industry, the company still lacked interaction with customers.

Bill Masters, Perception's president, challenged the company to **become fully interactive with customers**, both end-users and retailers, in a way that went beyond just reading surveys. Perception now has a professional call center, an interactive Web page, and most important, two technical field reps whose mission is to promote the sport of kayaking through education. The field reps, both skilled kayakers, travel around the country to train retail store personnel and demonstrate kayaking at festivals, competitions, and other special events.

Perception's education effort is working. Retailers are better trained to help kayak buyers, and fewer customers are calling in for answers to basic questions. In the other direction, the field reps get immediate feedback on customers' reactions to kayak comfort and even the latest colors. The reps' experience and enthusiasm also engages customers in a way that store employees can't. Coaching from a skilled trainer—and the opportunity to try any of 30 kayak designs—help people push past their doubts and get out on the water, paddling closer to a future kayak purchase.

Mail Bonding

Short of holding continuing-education classes nationwide, how can you ensure that your product will stay in use? Dr. Andrew Wang, cofounder of $1.5-million BayWare, in San Mateo, Calif., **dropped a postcard twice a month to his customers**, who were struggling to learn Japanese with the help of his first software offering, Power Japanese.

The neon-colored cards regaled the users—many of them business travelers—with tips on Japanese customs and pronunciations, printed in English and Japanese. "The postcards make us feel as though we are studying with the support of a group...they keep us motivated to keep learning," says a Power Japanese user. BayWare's cards kept arriving for a year—but only after a customer returned the registration card. A message flashed during installation, listing the rewards for registering. Some 60% of customers responded, which is about twice the norm.

Mailing out 5,000 postcards biweekly was a big job for BayWare's staff, but the $2,400 required to produce and mail monthly paled next to the payoff. "The purpose was to keep the language alive and keep in touch with customers," said Wang. "It's also turned out to be great for marketing."

A Stitch in Time

Diteck, a manufacturer of surge protectors, based in Largo, Fla., tracks the true cost of customer service independent of warranty costs or operating errors such as misshipments. By **analyzing customer-service costs**, the company has been able to reduce the direct product cost to the customer.

Robert Daugherty, vice-president and general manager, noticed that waiving the restocking charge for retailers who returned items after the 60-day return period was costing his company. The retailers had overstocked during the storm season and didn't want to carry extra inventory in the off-season. Since Diteck uses just-in-time manufacturing, a little retailer education solved the problem. The dealers now order smaller, more frequent shipments to prevent overstocks. As a result, everyone's costs are lower.

Good Cop, Bad Cop

Sometimes even long-standing customers have trouble paying bills. How can you collect on seriously late accounts without burning your bridges?

Loretta Johnson, controller of $12-million Industrial Machinery & Equipment, in Warren, Mich., never approaches late payers with, "Listen, deadbeat, I want my money." Instead, she calls customers and says, "Our bankers won't lend us any more money if I can't clear up your overdue account." Or, if customers have placed new orders, she tells them that Industrial wants to ship the product, but her bankers won't allow it until they apply some money to their oldest invoice. Johnson's **ask-for-help approach** has brought bad debt down to less than 1% of sales—and, better yet, it has kept relations with her customers cordial.

100
IDEA

Better Call to Confirm

You and your family get off the plane, pile into the rental car, and head out for vacation. Immediately you're faced with two problems: You can't remember the exact name or location of the hotel, and even if you did, you wouldn't know how to get there. This scenario is surprisingly common, according to Holly Boginis, general manager of the 99-room Lincoln Suites Hotel, located in Washington, D.C. And mailing a hotel brochure containing travel directions with reservation confirmations didn't solve the problem—people either don't read it or promptly misplace it. Other problems include requests for date changes (as many as 15% of guests) and no-shows.

Trying to avoid such hassles, the Lincoln Suites Hotel started a policy of **calling guests several days before their scheduled arrival date**. The front-desk staff person scheduled to be on duty when the guest arrives uses a checklist to review:

- Arrival and departure dates
- The number of people in the party
- Preferences for smoking or nonsmoking accommodation
- Directions to the hotel
- Special queries or requests, e.g., flowers in the room or tickets for events and tours

Guests like the personal connection, and the call eases travel anxiety by addressing last-minute concerns. When checking in, 25% of guests contacted through the program ask to speak to the person who made the confirmation call. As a result, the hotel has reduced the number of no-shows. And these days, the front desk is receiving fewer calls from lost vacationers.

Keep the Boss Quiet

In the start-up days of any company, it's perfectly logical for a CEO to double as chief salesperson. But once business starts to take off, it makes little sense to continue to play sales rep. Such was the case for Jim Genstein, CEO of In-a-Flash, a $2.6-million direct-mail company, located in Pittsburgh, that sells educational flash cards. After the ranks expanded to 12 employees, the boss **stopped taking orders** to concentrate on other aspects of the business. "I'm not allowed to talk to customers, because I don't have the time to be warm and fuzzy," he says.

"Some people will talk forever before making a choice over a $35 purchase. Eventually, I'll get to my boiling point and say, 'Sorry, I have to say good-bye now'—which is why my employees don't let me on the phone."

Customers now receive that warm and fuzzy feeling from In-a-Flash's inbound telemarketing customer-service agents. These agents let the customer linger longer on the phone line without upsetting the boss or the bottom line.

"Last year, each of our 10 million customers came in contact with approximately five SAS employees, and this contact lasted an average of 15 seconds each time. Thus, SAS is 'created' 50 million times a year, 15 seconds at a time. These 50 million 'moments of truth' are the moments that ultimately determine whether SAS will succeed or fail as a company. They are the moments when we must prove to our customers that SAS is their best alternative."

JAN CARLZON
former CEO of Scandinavian Airlines System (SAS),
in Stockholm, Sweden, and author of *Moments of Truth*
(Ballinger Publishing Company, 1987)

102
IDEA

Shhh! Lean Forward and Listen

How well you communicate with your customers is important. But making the sale might depend on your willingness to let your customers teach you a thing or two. "I tend to talk without listening, but big companies want you to **listen first**," says Jeff Hopmayer, CEO of Original American Scones, in Oak Park, Ill., which sold $5.9 million worth of baked goods last year.

At first, the more Hopmayer pushed his agenda with the big companies he approached, the slower things went. "One company spent $187,000 on focus groups to tell me it was okay to sell my scones," he says. "That drove me nuts." Hopmayer didn't win the orders until, he says, "I realized that by listening I could make improvements and make more sales."

First-Class Passenger Lounge

When you enter Direct Tire, based in the Boston area, you pass under a banner that reads, "We'll Fix It So It Brakes." That slogan, which owner Barry Steinberg wrote himself, provides barely a hint of what makes Direct Tire different from other automotive shops. The difference becomes apparent as soon as you step inside.

The **waiting room is as immaculate as a VIP lounge**. The magazines on the rack are current, with titles ranging from *Sports Illustrated* and *GQ* to *Vogue*. The coffee is freshly brewed. There are windows in every wall, allowing you to watch Direct Tire's technicians as they work. Looking around, you notice that **everyone is in uniform**. The managers and the salespeople wear shirts and ties with a baseball-style jacket that carries the company logo; everyone else has matching pants and T-shirts with the company name and slogan. Even the way people address you is different. "I've never heard so many *yes ma'ams* and *no ma'ams* in my life," says one customer who has been going to Direct Tire for years.

104
IDEA

'Tis Another Season

Sending Christmas cards used to be an effective way to plant your company's name before current and prospective customers. "People can't help feeling warmly about you," says Jack Kahl, president and CEO of Manco, a $150-million marketer of tapes, weather stripping, and mail supplies, located in Westlake, Ohio. But, notes Kahl, there is only so much warmth to go around.

These days, so many companies send greeting cards that yours can get lost in the shuffle. To stand out, Kahl has **added other, less "high-profile" holidays to his mailing roster**, such as Thanksgiving, St. Patrick's Day, and the Fourth of July.

To heighten interest, Manco has the cards designed in-house so they're different from run-of-the-mill greetings. "People open them up just to see what the next one will look like," says Kahl, whose mailing list includes close to 32,000 people. "It's a much more personal way to reach them."

For Whom the Toll's Free

When dialing up a company, no one likes to hear, "Sorry, that's not my department. Please hold while I transfer you." Such treatment kills customer service. So, in 1992, Deck House, a $17.5-million company that designs and manufactures post-and-beam houses, **dedicated an 800 phone line to customer service**. Once callers are satisfied, Deck House, located in Acton, Mass., keeps them on the line to conduct market research and obtain customer histories and referrals.

By the end of the customer-service line's first year, 2,018 calls had been logged in. Of the 800-line callers, 23% wanted to buy something; 10% required other sales information; 17% asked maintenance questions; and 12% asked miscellaneous questions. Approximately 25% were willing to pass on names of friends who might like to receive literature from Deck House. Fewer than 15% of the calls were complaints. What's more, the 800 line cut switchboard volume by almost 30%.

To make sure customers used the 800 line, CEO Michael Harris sent them plastic wallet cards touting the Deck House Owner Assistance Center, inviting customers to call toll-free for maintenance, sales, and warranty information. The service itself cost nothing: The company already had seven 800 lines, so Harris simply assigned one of them to the new customer-service number. The labor was supplied simply by reallocating existing personnel.

106 IDEA

Every Employee's a Service Rep

Each month, Restek, an $18-million manufacturer of lab-equipment parts, located in Bellefonte, Pa., phones 200 to 300 customers as part of the company's **call-back program**. Many call-back recipients are first-time buyers that customer-service reps are eager to interview, asking questions such as "Did the product arrive undamaged? Is it performing to expectations? Any ideas for new products?" Restek also contacts customers who have returned products and those who haven't ordered anything for at least one year.

The call-back program gives Restek the direct word on why customers don't come back, as well as feedback on new products. "When customers complain about a product, the follow-up call might be made by the people who manufactured or tested it," explains Neil Mosesman, Restek's product incubation team manager, "so they really want to know why something didn't work. And employees feel they need to bend over backward to fix the problem. They can't simply say that a customer doesn't know what he's talking about."

Stamp Out Debt

When you send out a past-due statement, it makes for a nasty follow-up call," says Thom Holden, cofounder of a six-employee design firm, in Media, Pa., with annual billings of more than $1 million. But a little humor can certainly help to melt the ice.

Holden and his partner, Dave Bell, created a "spread the wealth" **rubber stamp for late notices**. The stamp's bright-green logo depicts two men playing tug-of-war with a dollar bill. "It warms up the conversation when I call," Holden says.

He and Bell came up with the idea when they started Thom & Dave Marketing Design in 1989, and they needed ways to improve cash flow and speed up accounts receivable. With the exception of one account, bad debt hasn't been a problem for Thom & Dave, and their clients appreciate the opportunity for a chuckle.

"One often hears the remark
'He talks too much,' but
when did anyone last
hear the criticism
'He listens too much'?"

NORMAN R. AUGUSTINE
chairman of Lockheed Martin Corporation,
in Bethesda, Md., and author of *Augustine's Laws*
(Penguin, 1987)

Make Errors Headline News

Successful firms learn from their mistakes if they're careful not to sweep errors under the rug. "Unfortunately, many customers mistakenly think they do us a favor by not reporting problems," says Diane Hathaway, president of Industrial Traffic Consultants (ITC), a $3-million logistics consulting firm that manages freight payments for customers, located in Longwood, Fla. The customer may not want to seem like a complainer, or may view the error as too small to report.

One way to encourage customers to complain is to show them how serious you are about tracking and reducing mistakes. That's why ITC **publishes quarterly error rates**, by department, **on the front page of the customer newsletter**, which appears every other month. Explanations are provided for negative trends. For example, one department's increase in errors was attributable to a software upgrade. Customers are also sent error ratios for their accounts on a monthly basis.

The high-visibility error reporting tells customers that ITC is concerned with prevention, and its low error rate promotes the firm's image. Reporting mistakes also creates a good-spirited department rivalry, without discouraging ITC's 35 employees from reporting complaints. Some error reports count toward winning cash prizes in the employee suggestion contest, and a continuous-improvement orientation, backed up by profit sharing, produces committed workers.

ITC's high-visibility error tracking system has paid off. In three years, total department errors have decreased from more than 1% to less than 1%, with three departments showing rates below 0.1% in 1996.

Label Us Meticulous

When work orders don't reflect customer needs, product rejection rates rise. Unfortunately, customers don't always have the technical knowledge to convey precise product specifications. At Ampersand, a custom-label company, located in Garden Grove, Calif., a client who orders cake labels, but neglects to mention a flash-freezing process, could end up buying labels with an adhesive guaranteed to fail in that application.

Ampersand's solution is improved communication with customers by **making the order confirmation process a meaningful exercise**. Instead of sending out a superficial order confirmation for "peach shampoo labels" that arrives after the product has been shipped, vice-president Paulette Carnes faxes order confirmations with all necessary job specifications, such as adhesives, substrates, and machine applications. A support person calls the client every 24 hours until the details are reviewed.

Customers must sign off on the confirmation order, which forces them to stop and think about all aspects of the job. To save time, they don't have to create a separate purchase order—they simply write the P. O. number on their order confirmation.

First-time customers sometimes think, "Why do you guys keep sending paperwork and calling?" But, says Carnes, Ampersand catches potential errors all the time, and new customers soon learn that this process is in their own best interest. Ampersand's material rejection rates are less than 0.5%—compared to an industry average of 3%. And the extra communication and reduced errors build long-term relationships.

110
IDEA

Use Honey, Not Vinegar

Mike Watts, co-owner and vice-president of Professional Resources, a data-processing-services company, based in Overland Park, Kans., uses personal service to facilitate collection efforts. Watts's collection strategy departs from the usual techniques and centers on **getting to know each client's accounts-payable clerk**.

Whenever his company sends an invoice, Watts follows up by telephoning the person responsible for payables. "I explain that I want to make certain they're happy with our service and that our invoice is clear to them. I'll try to get to know them a little bit—after all, they're people too, with families, hobbies, and weekend plans. Once every month or so, I'll call to check in with them. I sometimes even follow up with a visit. Very few vendors ever take the time to do this, but people appreciate it."

Results have been impressive: A typical invoice from Professional Resources takes 24 days to collect, compared with the national average of 42 days. Best of all, reports Watts, no one has ever taken advantage of his friendly demeanor to slow down a bill payment. "Because we've got a rapport, they understand our financial needs."

111
IDEA

Let Your Clients Do the Talking

The start of a client relationship is the riskiest phase, according to Dana Hutchins, president and creative director of Image Works, a multimedia production company, located in Portland, Maine. Because mismatched expectations are common, communicating with prospective customers to understand their needs and to set expectations is critical. Hutchins makes sure to let the customers ask the questions rather than the other way around.

When pitching new clients, most companies lead the conversation, asking questions to identify client needs. Image Works uses a different approach in its pitch. It starts by **creating a customized Web page for each prospective customer**. To get the customer thinking, the site highlights previously created multimedia projects that are relevant to the customer's industry. Prospective customers are invited to ask the company questions once they've seen the Web site. The results are phenomenal. Questions flow freely: "How did you do that?" "How does this type of media fit into our strategy?" "What are the bottom-line results of this endeavor?" "Can you complete something like this for me in a month?"

"Customer-led dialogue generates an understanding of the client's needs and sets clear expectations," says Hutchins. "The up-front effort to get customers talking certainly results in a smoother project start and a shorter project completion time."

112
IDEA

Keep in Touch

Are your customers frustrated when they can't reach you? Do they have to be transferred three times before reaching the right person? Here's how three different businesses keep the lines of communication open with customers.

Telecom Project Assistance, a telecommunications consulting firm, in Mountain View, Calif., provides customers with a list of every executive's title, job description, and direct phone number. **Customers reach the person they want without call screening**. If the executive is not available, the customer may leave a voice mail message—or, at the touch of a key, connect to someone else.

Intech Construction, a building company in Philadelphia, believes customers should be able to reach employees whenever there's a problem—day or night. The customer receives contact numbers for every employee on the customer's project: office telephone, fax, digital pager, mobile telephone, and home telephone.

APS Technologies, a Kansas City, Mo., provider of computer products and support, thinks customers should be able to contact the company however they want. To that end, the company offers several communication vehicles for its clients: a toll-free telephone number, a fax number, postal mail, E-mail, an interactive Web site, online services and bulletin boards, trade shows, and in-person user groups.

Love from the Assembly Line

Open communication is a hallmark of the 300 employees in the plants of Super Sack Manufacturing Corp., a producer of bulk containers, in Fannin County, Tex. Production workers are organized into self-directed work teams dedicated to specific customers. Team members meet customers when they visit the plant, or they may travel to the customer's location to learn about product usage and gain an understanding of emergency situations that may arise.

"Teams are mature enough to see the business perspective and take ownership for their work," says Nancy Cline, director of quality. "**Production teams communicate directly with customers**, and we encourage them. Team members initiated more than 30 letters to customers last year. We address, stamp, and mail the letters without changing them." A management cover letter is occasionally added to reinforce the company's commitment to the customer.

"One letter explained why an order was late—the production team wanted to give the information firsthand. Another team, whose orders were slim because the customer was going through a transition, wrote to ask if there was anything they could do to help with the transition. Many of the letters included suggestions that would make the team's work easier, increase productivity, and thus produce cost savings for the customer."

"Customer response to the letters has been 'wow,' " says Cline. "A letter from a production team is surprising because people are used to management-to-management communications. Cross-level communication shows customers that teams are buying into the plan and are dedicated to the customer."

Gosh, That Was Fast

Customers think they wait in line longer than they actually do. Jerome Gravel uses three **techniques to make service seem faster** at his Subway sandwich shop, a franchise business, in Portland, Maine.

- *Eye contact.* The nine employees at Gravel's $260,000 operation are trained to make eye contact and acknowledge the customer's presence within three seconds of entry. Gravel believes that when customers feel welcomed instead of ignored, they are less likely to focus on the wait.

- *Wait-time estimate.* When there is a line, employees give the customer an accurate estimate of the length of the wait. Waiting seems longer when one doesn't know how long it will be.

- *Customer involvement.* Customers indicate what they want as the sandwiches are made, rather than providing all details up front. "When customers are involved throughout the process, they don't see themselves as waiting," emphasizes Gravel. "The customer also has a greater perception that we're trying to do exactly what they want and care how the product turns out."

The perception of fast service translates into repeat business. Within 60 days of implementing these practices, sales rose 10% from the previous year, and that figure has increased to 20%. Gravel believes that at least half of the increase is due to the perception of faster service.

Keeping Tabs on Expectations

The concept is simple: **Match customer expectations with yours**. Making it happen is more difficult.

Managing expectations is essential for Fourth Dimension Software (FDS), a company that develops customized software solutions. Up to three years may elapse between a sale and project completion, says Chris McAllister, vice-president of customer service for the $12-million Redwood City, Calif., company. Here's how McAllister manages its customers' expectations:

- *Create a realistic prototype.* FDS provides mock-up screens that the client's users play with to understand how the software will function. "When their suggestions are incorporated into the final design, they become proud to accept the finished product, rather than reluctant," says McAllister. The prototype also gives the purchaser something concrete to show executives how the money is being spent.

- *Provide an executive overview in addition to product specifications.* "Top management isn't going to read 600 pages of technical specifications," observes McAllister. "They will read a 10- to 40-page overview, with diagrams, of what the system will do."

- *Review letters to customers.* "No matter who writes what, have someone else check it," says McAllister. The issue isn't grammar, but tone and clarity. Is it technically accurate? Does it set clear expectations for the nontechnical reader?

The prototypes, executive overviews, and letter reviews are worth the effort. "Since we began in 1981, 100% of our projects have reached their objectives and gone live," he says. "The key is managing expectations."

Framing the Decision

Customers like to think of themselves as smart shoppers. General Optical Co., in Cambridge, Mass., believes that knowledgeable shoppers are more likely to be satisfied with their purchases. "If a customer wants to buy eyeglass frames for the style or brand name, that's fine as long as it's an informed decision," says store owner Ron Arslanian.

His employees often take eyeglass frames apart in front of the customer to illustrate the finer points of frame construction. For example, the delicate construction of a stylish frame may not be suitable for a customer's lifestyle, occupation, or prescription. Arslanian further helps customers with the decision process by letting them take a couple of frames home for a second opinion.

According to Arslanian, few salespeople in the industry actually **help customers understand what they're buying**. He's convinced that General Optical's educational approach explains why the business has 10,000 active clients, with 50% of business generated from repeat customers and 35% from referrals.

117
IDEA

Direct Line to Top Service

Customer feedback is the raw material needed to improve customer service. To give customers an opportunity to offer feedback, the Fire House Car Wash, an automated, full-service car wash in Denver, installed a **bright red phone labeled "Hot Line to the Owner"** in the waiting room. About 10 customers a week use the phone to speak with owner Bill Kuntzler.

"Customers love the phone," says Kuntzler, "because it's a direct line to me anytime they have something to report. Eighty percent of calls are from people who just want to say thanks because we offer free coffee or because employees were extremely polite and did a great job. Some of the calls come from kids in the waiting room playing with the phone. I'm always pleased to get calls from customers, and if playing with the phone entertains waiting children, all the better." If Kuntzler is unable to take the call, an empathetic message encourages customers to leave a message or, if they prefer, to see the receptionist. Kuntzler responds to all messages within 24 hours.

The 75-employee operation washes 4,000 cars a week. Its success, says Kuntzler, is due to its commitment to customers.

My One and Only

Peter Bull of Cherry Hill, N.J., didn't want his customers to feel the frustration he feels when talking with a customer-service rep who doesn't know him or his situation. At his company, Taurus Packaging and Display, a provider of point-of-purchase advertising displays, **each customer is assigned to one customer-service rep**, and arrangements are made for the two to meet, if possible.

With an assigned rep, the customer has an advocate within Taurus. This is someone who will give the salesperson on the account a well-timed nudge rather than just stick another note in an out box. The customer-service rep and salesperson on an account form a team that backs each other up. Working with specific clients is more fulfilling for the service reps, too. Team camaraderie develops, and the rep feels instrumental in the success of a finished project.

Bull's strategy also pays off in customer retention. Customers say they like the personal, efficient service and have strong relationships with their reps. "When I phone customers to see how everything's going, they often say they are ready to place another order. I offer to take the order, but they say no, they'd rather place it with Danielle in customer service. It's not that I'm going to muff the order, it's that they have a good relationship with their rep," Bull observes. "The superior service provided by the assigned reps is one reason our sales have grown from zero to $12 million in six years."

Calling All Extensions

Picture this: You call up to order some winter underwear and, instead of making you fidget on hold while elevator music blares in your ear, someone answers right away. It may sound unusual, but that's what happens at WinterSilks, a mail-order apparel business, in Middleton, Wis.

If a WinterSilks telemarketer isn't able to answer a phone within 16 seconds, the call is automatically redirected to the order department (which temporarily stops processing mail orders). If that department's lines are busy, the call rolls over to the customer-service department or even further along to the general administrative office. **Anyone in the company, including the president, will take the call** so that the customer doesn't have to wait.

John Reindl, vice-president of operations, believes that being there for customers is also good for employees. "Working directly with a customer reminds us how our personal responsibility translates into service, one customer at a time," he says.

"Don't fix the product,
fix the customer. Educating
the customer is one of the
best—and least expensive—
solutions available."

JOHN GOODMAN
president of TARP Inc.,
in Arlington, Va.

120
IDEA

Don't Hesitate to Wake Us

Want to let your customers know how committed you are to serving them? For years, J.W. Kisling, the CEO of Multiplex Inc., a St. Louis maker of beverage-dispensing equipment for the food-service industry, has **listed the home phone numbers of the company's 16 directors and officers in its catalog**. Next to the list is a suggested contact to call in case of emergency. "The secret," confides Kisling, "is we only get a couple of calls a year. But seeing it in writing impresses the hell out of our customers."

Multiplex doesn't limit its customer-service commitment to senior management, however. When Kisling gives tours of the facility, he invariably stops at a workstation to chat with one of the company's 120 factory employees. "It impresses a customer to see that our employees can explain what's going on around them. Everyone's a salesperson here," he says.

121

IDEA

No Leaks in the Pipeline

Service providers are always looking for ways to distinguish themselves from competitors. Lorie Spaulding, office manager at Paul J. Halstead Plumbing and Heating, based in Littleton, Mass., set her husband's business apart by promoting fast emergency response.

Like many plumbers, electricians, and other tradespeople who find themselves on the road each day, Halstead used a beeper. When a customer called, his beeper would sound, and he'd have to find a phone to return the call. That delay alone put off callers who were having an emergency; they'd just call another plumber. What's more, if Halstead was stuck in a crawl space on a difficult job, he wouldn't be able to call back for hours. And that cost him routine business, as well.

So when Spaulding joined the company, she **hired an answering service that paged her** when an emergency call came in, so that someone could talk to the caller immediately. The quick response "reassured people and definitely kept us from losing business," she says. Spaulding also placed ads in the local paper and phone book, which read, "10-minute response to all emergency calls" and "24-hour phone."

As a result, Spaulding says many customers call her first when they need a plumber. And keeping the promise has built a loyal clientele for Halstead Plumbing: "About 75% of our business now consists of return customers," she says.

Out of Town, Not Out of Touch

George Matarazzo wanted to get away from the city. So he closed down his high-growth, high-profile landscape-architecture firm and started a new solo business, Matarazzo Land Planning Consultants—a company he runs out of a barn on his 80-acre farm in Wilmot Flat, N.H.

Matarazzo's business is national, and it depends on contacts and a reputation developed over many years. But he had one problem: In Wilmot Flat, some of Matarazzo's old customers couldn't find him. People who knew him would occasionally call Concord, N.H.—the home of the now-defunct Matarazzo Design—looking for a company that wasn't there.

Matarazzo's solution was simple. For a modest monthly base fee, he **maintains a telephone listing at his old location**, using his old Matarazzo Design name, in addition to the new Wilmot Flat number for Matarazzo Land Planning. People who call Directory Assistance in Concord get the Concord number, which automatically transfers the call to the Wilmot Flat line. Matarazzo picks up the long-distance charges for that transfer; he estimates that he never pays more than $25 a month for the entire service. And, in a business in which a call from an old client can yield months of work, that's a price Matarazzo is willing to pay.

IDEA

A Line for All Speakers

ere's a way to get customers to speak their minds: Set up a **24-hour hot line to record confidential messages**, give it a folksy name such as Speakline, and promote it on company stationery, invoices, and "How'd-We-Do?" cards.

AVCA Corp. did, and customers of the $25-million engineering and architectural service firm, in Maumee, Ohio, are warming up to the switch-board-free line.

Some two dozen customers—about half of AVCA's active clients—call Speakline each month, often to leave project-related questions. They also inquire about bills, make suggestions, and praise jobs well done. The line is especially convenient for customers who don't have time to write, don't know who should field their questions, and don't want to play telephone tag for days.

AVCA president Dean Diver spends two to three hours a week monitoring the messages. If he can't get back to a customer within 24 hours, he sends a note to explain.

The company started Speakline because of the response rate on customer comment cards. "We received a 35% return rate on those cards. So we knew our customers wanted to talk."

124

IDEA

Fiddler on the Roof

T&K Roofing Co.'s new customer-service department—complete with its own special truck, logo, and uniform—grew out of a need. Every night around closing time a customer called with an emergency. Working under bright lights and at overtime rates, a crew would scramble out and fix the problem. T&K's managers began to analyze how they could better prepare for such service calls.

Kurt Tjelmeland, vice-president of the company, located in Ely, Iowa, sensed an opportunity. How customers feel depends on how well the staff manages moments of truth—specific encounters and turning points—during which customers form solid opinions about a company. T&K, Tjelmeland argued, could **turn emergencies into truly magic moments**.

So far, the concept has required some fine-tuning. Given their often-unpredictable schedules, the service reps found themselves falling behind, irritating customers. As a result, many of the service reps now carry cellular phones. If nobody's home when they arrive, they hang doorknob signs to let customers know they came and looked at the roof. "We'd get calls saying, 'Your man never showed up,'" says Tjelmeland. "I figured, these things work for hotels, so why not try them?"

The More You Check, the More You Sell

When you don't sell your product directly to the end-user, the retailer is your customer. Koss Corp., a Milwaukee-based leading maker of stereo headphones and speakers, responds by **helping the retailer sell** Koss's products. During a lull in sales calls, John Koss Jr., vice-president of sales, goes on a tour.

First stop: Wal-Mart. Apparently outranked by Sony, Koss headphones have been relegated to a bottom rung on the slat wall. "We have plans to change that," Koss says, tidying up the display.

The nearby Target store is brighter than Wal-Mart. But Koss's best-selling $24.99 headphones, the TD-61 model, are out of stock. Worse, three pegs are wasted on a model that sells poorly.

At Best Buy, Koss's demo pair of $39 computer speakers doesn't work. John Koss fiddles with wires to no avail. "If something's not working, we want to know right away so we can replace it," he says, walking off to find a manager.

To remedy such problems, Koss has appealed to at least one superstore "rebuyer" (the buyer's assistant). Some vendors rely on the folks who actually stock shelves, the rack jobbers, to make things right. Few sales reps will play housekeeper, but the best make spot checks. "The buyer might say that product's not selling," says Lee Adams, a Koss rep in Bedford, Tex. "And I can say, 'That's because it's in the back room.' I gain credibility, and the buyer fixes the problem."

126 IDEA

Just the Fax, Please

The fax machine is the undisputed favorite business tool of international executives when communicating with their foreign customers. In short, fax machines provide proof of receipt, they set forth all agreement terms in writing, and they're impervious to time zones. However, Richard Koehler, president of an international marketing firm who also teaches classes on international business for the M.B.A. program at the University of Houston, warns fax users to be careful. "People using English as a second language are more comfortable sticking with the facts: the terms and vocabulary they work with on a daily basis such as items available, price rates, and terms of delivery."

According to Koehler, miscommunication is a key hazard of doing international business. "The fax helps streamline delivery of information, but **precise language in fax correspondence** is one of the best services a firm can provide their overseas customers," says Koehler, who cautions that friendly American colloquialisms, acronyms, and slang terms only muddy the waters.

"One of my seminar students couldn't understand why it took a customer an entire week to respond to an 'ASAP' request he had made for some documents," says Koehler. "The foreign client might not have known what 'ASAP' stood for, and even if he did understand the term, he might have interpreted it differently. In the United States, 'ASAP' means drop everything, but in another country, it may mean 'get it done by the end of the week.' It's better to specify dates and times and not leave important facts open to interpretation."

127
IDEA

Head-On Cooperation

Many contractors run and hide if a property manager calls with a complaint. But Clem Majerus, founder of GTW Construction, in Irving, Tex., holds a **"partner intervention" session to address jobs that have run amok**—a rare customer service in the industry, and one that has fueled growth of the company from $9 million in 1996 to $25 million in 1997.

An intervention works like this: Say one of GTW's typical customers, a property manager, complains about paint peeling at a site that recently had been renovated. Rather than take endless messages from the customer and put off honoring the warranty, GTW sends down the supervisor who worked on the site, as well as a representative from the paint manufacturer. Together with the property manager, they analyze why the paint is peeling and determine who is responsible for the damage. At most, such a meeting would cost $500, but it typically costs $100 to $200.

Everyone's a lot happier that high-priced lawyers don't have to be called in to resolve the problem. "We try to show an equal amount of interest in the problem the customer perceives it to be," says Majerus. Clearly the policy is effective: "The sales are primarily coming from our existing customer base," adds Majerus.

128 IDEA

Signed, Sealed, and Delivered

When a customer returns an unsatisfactory product to a company, and a replacement must be shipped, any profit earned on the sale dwindles—along with any goodwill the customer has for the firm. For Bay Cast, a specialty manufacturer of steel castings, taking rejects from its international customers isn't even an option. Because castings can easily weigh 40,000 pounds, the transportation charges make returns prohibitive. "We'd have to send someone over to the customer to repair it, if it could even be done at all," says Scott Holman Sr., CEO of the Bay City, Mich., company, whose overseas customers accounted for approximately 30% of its $15 million in revenues in 1997.

As a result, Bay Cast **refuses to ship an order until a customer or third-party representative for the customer visits** the foundry to inspect the order and sign for it. The policy was developed out of a worst-case-scenario planning meeting. "We are a conservative company," says Holman. "We always look at the worst that can happen to a customer's order before taking on a job."

129

IDEA

Go Write to the Top

There are moments when customers simply want to let off some steam and be heard by someone who matters," says Hartley Peavey, founder and CEO of Peavey Electronics, in Meridian, Miss. One of the best communication tools his company has developed to keep in touch with its 1,400 dealers in the United States is the Co-Act (short for cooperation and action) program. Each dealer receives **stationery and a stack of postage-paid envelopes addressed to the CEO's attention**, so that customers can fire off missives in the heat of the moment to complain about service or salespeople, suggest how to improve products, or flag billing problems.

Peavey responds personally to each letter within two weeks and answers about half a dozen letters a day, detailing the action taken on behalf of the customer. If any technical issues are beyond his grasp, he holds a briefing meeting with the appropriate employees.

Says Peavey, "A lot of companies have survey forms, but they don't go to the top, and the ones that do are usually answered by a form letter. I never have used a form letter and never will. And I do not use a signature stamp. I personally sign each one. These letters serve as a source of ideas for product improvements, a way to keep track of our employees' performance, and, most important, a way to keep customer relations positive."

130
IDEA

The Customer Isn't Always Right

Challenging customers' assumptions about what they should be purchasing from your company may sound like more of a hassle than a method of servicing them. After all, the customer is always right, right? "Wrong," says Carol Laskey, founder of Cahoots!, a marketing and communications firm, based in Boston.

Rather than slave away to a buyer's every whim, Laskey holds **preorder conferences with customers and prospects** to ensure, for example, that the standard eight-page brochure is really the best way for a client to develop its corporate identity and reach its customers. "It's easy to take an order, but adding this extra step to the order process helps eliminate a lot of potential disappointments before the meter starts ticking," Laskey says.

Laskey also offers her expertise to help her clients save money. Because her customers aren't marketing communications specialists, they may not know the best way to leverage their marketing dollars to reach their goals. "One customer wanted to spend his entire marketing budget on a brochure, when the sales cycle for the product stretched to five years," says Laskey. "Instead, we guided him toward a long-term strategy that involved 17 components, including video materials and print publications."

Mapping Eliminates Mystery

Where's my order?" is perhaps a customer's most frequently asked question. And how a company answers this question is a hallmark of its customer service. At Bay Cast, a manufacturer of specialty steel castings, in Bay City, Mich., customers get the answer before work on an order commences.

When a job begins, each customer receives **a detailed "road map" displaying the various manufacturing steps the order will take and the time it will require**. "You have to check the road signs along the way," says CEO Scott Holman Sr. "At weekly production meetings we look at where in the process the order is—every single casting is discussed. Then, after the meeting, we fax customers with multiple orders a weekly update on their orders' status. Some customers may have a couple of dozen orders going through at a time, and this tracking process makes it easy for them to follow our progress."

Giving customers the "big picture" in advance allows them to rest easy, knowing what's happening between the time they place an order and the week they receive it. As a result, Bay Cast employees are able to focus on filling the order rather than managing it. The company averages an on-time delivery rate of 99% in an industry whose standard is less than 60%. This phenomenal delivery rate helped drive sales from $3 million in 1987 to $15 million in 1997.

Lowering the Language Barrier

Finding a good interpreter is crucial to providing foreign customers with services such as equipment-orientation seminars. Marty McCann, an audio engineer for Peavey Electronics, a guitar and sound-system company employing approximately 2,200 people in the United States, has traveled the globe for more than 10 years teaching sound professionals and music distributors. Here are McCann's **pointers for finding the right interpreter** for your specific needs:

1) Make sure an interpreter knows the vocabulary for your specific product. "Once I had an interpreter who was in tears in front of a class because she didn't have a background in audio engineering." Just in case, have a local management person on hand to assist. "Host-country techies may not be as fluent in English, but they have more insight into the material."

2) Get someone who's persnickety. "It's a good sign if your interpreter stops and asks you to clarify things before continuing." Have dinner with your interpreter the day before the presentation to familiarize him or her with your speech and mannerisms.

3) Instruct the interpreter to focus on your material and not the language itself. "One interpreter I used, an English teacher, was trying to make my speech grammatically correct rather than communicate the material—and she was telling *me* how to correct my English!"

4) Use your local contacts and distributors as leads for qualified interpreters. Sometimes they can tap a customer who speaks English well. McCann's company tries to find someone already fluent with the vocabulary and interested in the product, with whom it may also strike a barter arrangement for services.

V

"The worst thing you can do
is to be superficial about
measuring customer satisfaction.
Customers are bright. They see
right through the hypocrisy
and actually devalue
your product or service."

SHEILA KESSLER
president of Competitive Edge, in Fountain Valley, Calif.,
and author of *Measuring and Managing
Customer Satisfaction: Going for the Gold*
(Quality Press, 1996)

A+ for Homework

The secret to meeting client needs is doing your homework, says Craig DeLuca, president of Executive Perspectives (EP), a 40-employee management training firm, located in Brookline, Mass., that bills close to $10 million per year. EP goes the extra mile to understand and meet customer needs by self-imposing an extra step in the product design process.

Before the firm accepts a job, an EP sales associate must submit a written report answering every question on a 24-page **sales/design checklist**. Comprehensive answers to questions such as "What is the organization's plan?" and "Is the client unclear how it will measure results?" make it possible to design an optimal training product. Customers are asked to sign off on the specifications at the beginning and middle of the design process. If EP can't deliver the best possible product, it refers the business to a competitor.

Although the checklist requires more up-front work for EP, the effort is worthwhile, DeLuca says, because you don't have to cross your fingers once the product is delivered and hope the customer is happy. With 70% of revenue coming from follow-up projects, and less than 5% voluntary customer attrition over a 13-year history, it's clear that customers are satisfied.

Don't Forget the Quiet Ones!

Customer surveys may call attention to problems only after the fact, and ongoing demands from new and vocal customers may drown out a loyal, but silent, majority. How can you meet their needs?

The Kansas City office of Harte-Hanks Communications, a provider of database marketing systems, listens to the silence. This $30-million business unit formally **reviews its stewardship of each account** once a year. All personnel on an account discuss all aspects of serving that client. "The process is effective at uncovering areas where we could do better," says Henry Lammers, vice-president of marketing. "We have time to improve before the customer complains or leaves." For example, a review of the Similac infant formula account led to the addition of Internet access for customer service. Sometimes account reviews reveal cross-selling opportunities.

Harte-Hanks' annual reviews also allow employees to identify their favorite (and least favorite) aspects of working on an account. When possible, they adjust work to accommodate employee preferences. After all, happier employees are an important step toward happier clients.

135
IDEA

Drink the Competitor's Water

Is your service up to snuff? What aspect of service should you improve next? To answer these questions, Pure Water Corp., located in Seattle, routinely asks five of its 35,000 current customers to buy from a competitor. Pure Water reimburses the customer for the cost of the competitor's water in return for feedback on its service.

Allen Bechtel, president of the $10-million company, prefers to **use current customers to evaluate the competition** instead of hiring professional mystery shoppers. He believes that asking customers to buy from the competition can serve as an opportunity for Pure Water to improve its product, rather than threaten its revenue.

When customers reported that one competitor offered better value, Bechtel listened carefully. The competitor's price was higher, but more frequent deliveries meant fewer bottles underfoot. In response, Bechtel designed a delivery schedule and pricing structure offering greater value to Pure Water customers.

Bechtel is careful in selecting customers for the program, so he hasn't lost a single one. Loyal customers who are innovative in their own businesses like the idea of participating in an experiment. Indeed, the experience ends up solidifying the customer's relationship with Pure Water.

Make a List, Check It Quarterly

Customer-satisfaction surveys were a good tool in the 1980s, but now they are overused and less helpful, says Kent Lane, vice-president of post-sales operations at Metrix, a service-management software company, based in Waukesha, Wis. Customers inundated with lengthy surveys don't respond carefully, and generally you only hear from folks who are really happy or really unhappy. Surveys are not enough if your goal is to make every customer a reference site for future business.

Lane's solution is to **rely on employees to assess customer satisfaction**. Although Metrix is in a high-tech business, it returns to old-fashioned talking and listening. Each client is assigned a team comprised of an executive, a consultant, a support person, and the salesperson. During quarterly meetings, the team uses a checklist to assess customer satisfaction:

Is the customer's implementation of our product a success? Does the customer retain a support agreement with us? Will this customer be a reference site for prospective customers? What is the customer's temperament when we make goodwill calls? Are there new managers in place who need to be resold on Metrix? Is the implementation process workable in terms of switching software?

Use of the checklist allows for baseline comparisons over time. The checklist also serves as a tangible reminder of the issues employees should continually focus on when interacting with clients. By making employees responsible for assessment, Metrix encourages employees to take more initiative to satisfy customers. The approach works, judging by one of the checklist's measures of success: An enviable 95% of Metrix customers have signed annual support contracts. Revenues have grown from $1.5 million to $20 million from 1993 to 1997.

That's a Good Question

Salespeople talk with customers frequently, so they should be able to funnel information on client needs back to headquarters. However, it doesn't usually work that way in practice because sales reps don't ask the right questions. "A typical courtesy call from a sales rep goes something like: 'How ya doing? Are there any problems?' The response is always a quick no—if there had been a problem, they would have called. You don't learn about your customers," observes Michael Karpoff, president of First Priority Group (FPG), a $33-million company, based in Plainview, N.Y.

Karpoff, whose $14-million company manages collision repair for corporate fleets, now requires his sales reps to **ask customers a piercing question** once or twice a quarter. A good question focuses the customer's attention on one specific aspect of FPG's business operation: "If you could add, delete, or change anything on the driver response card so as to help you get better information, what would that be?" Sometimes questions explore a specific dimension of customer satisfaction: "What special effort has our customer-service representative taken on your driver's behalf?" The increased specificity of the questions has increased the thoughtfulness of the replies.

If a client doesn't offer any feedback, the sales rep is trained to continue the education process by providing information on the question topic. Sales reps are also required to review with their clients the results of traditional surveys and tentative conclusions about service improvements. This approach works so well for Karpoff that he no longer sees the need for formal, in-depth interviews with clients.

138

IDEA

Filling Out the Envelope

Customer feedback is essential, but getting customers to respond to surveys is a challenge. Home Delivery Incontinent Supply (HDIS), a 35-employee mail-order company, located in Olivette, Mo., **prints survey questions directly on remittance envelopes** sent with customer orders. The survey appears either on a perforated portion of the sealing flap (the customer tears it off and encloses it) or on the back of the envelope, which has an extra-long sealing flap to cover the answers.

Survey questions ask customers to rate the telephone representative, the product selection, the speed and accuracy of the shipment, and the company overall. To keep customers from becoming bored, the closed-ended questions are periodically replaced by a request for open-ended feedback or by discount offers for ancillary products such as air fresheners.

All open-ended suggestions are followed up with a phone call or letter. Open-ended questions are particularly effective with sensitive items like incontinence products, says HDIS marketer Angela Farrell, because customers are more likely to express thoughts about them in writing, rather than on the phone. The company is quickly alerted to disliked product changes and obtains valuable insight on serving customers. For example, in response to their suggestions, HDIS gives customers access to staff who have expert knowledge about incontinence, and it prints its catalog with enlarged type to make it easier for the elderly to read.

Tremendous response rates are achieved—around 80%—because the survey is short, noticeable, and returned with payments. HDIS can track trends without the lag associated with yearly surveys. Also, ongoing surveys provide a constant stream of positive feedback that rewards and motivates the staff.

Skip the Third Party

Four years ago, Franks and Son, a long-distance truckload carrier, based in Big Cabin, Okla., jumped on the bandwagon of surveying customer satisfaction by hiring an outside firm to conduct a phone survey. "We quickly found out that our customers didn't want a third party between us," says Kathrena Franks, CFO of the $16-million company. She heard back from 20% of customers with remarks such as "Who are these strangers?" and "If you want to know how you're doing, call us directly!"

Now the company stays in close contact with customers and solicits feedback with a letter of appreciation accompanied by a small gift. "The letters are written as poems that give our customers a laugh," says Franks, "and 50% percent of customers respond with notes or phone calls."

For a small operation like hers with close ties to customers, Franks feels that the **best way to gather feedback is a personal approach**, which makes relationships even stronger. This advice may not be true for all businesses, but it does make sense to find out how your customers prefer to be surveyed on your service.

Finding Hidden Expectations

Many customers aren't able to articulate their expectations clearly and, as a result, end up disappointed with the service they receive. Ripon Community Printers, a 350-employee company, located in Ripon, Wis., **uncovers hidden expectations by interviewing new customers about their experiences with previous service providers**. Customers are asked to provide a sample of their previous printer's work and comment on its quality. A Ripon customer-service representative reviews the sample with the customer to learn what is and is not acceptable.

"Knowing what customers want as early as possible is key in getting the job done right," says Tom Montag, customer-service manager. Understanding what they weren't pleased with in the past reveals their true expectations. "Providing great service means no surprises for you or your customers when the job is done," Montag says.

Looking for hidden expectations has paid off. Customer surveys show that 96.1% of customers feel Ripon's services meet or exceed their needs, and 76.5% feel the service is better than that of previous print vendors.

"You can go out and academically study the market and draw some conclusions about what your customers want, but at a certain point you need a sanity check on all your assumptions."

KATHLEEN E. SYNNOTT
vice-president of worldwide postal affairs,
Pitney Bowes Inc., in Stamford, Conn.

Smooth As Silk

WinterSilks, a $45-million mail-order company that specializes in silk apparel, tries to keep customer-service quality on a par with its merchandise. Here are some of its tips:

&. **Give everyone customer contact**. To keep the entire staff close to the customer, the Middleton, Wis., company requires all 300 employees, including senior management, to take a minimum of 50 phone orders annually.

&. **"Mystery shop" the competition**. WinterSilks employees continually shop competitors' catalogs anonymously. One customer-service representative places the call while several others monitor it. After the call, the group evaluates the competitor's representative on product knowledge, available information, and attitude. When the merchandise arrives, WinterSilks' merchandising department evaluates the actual item, while the shipping staff studies package presentation. Next, WinterSilks employees send the merchandise back, examining the returns system and the processing time. John Reindl, vice-president of operations, says the company has made numerous changes based on the results, from personalizing its thank-you cards to improving gift-certificate presentation.

&. **Circulate customer feedback**. WinterSilks distributes a monthly top-10 list of customer comments—both good and bad—to all staff members. The list helps employees recognize simple ways to increase customer satisfaction.

142
IDEA

First Ask, Then Follow Up

Since the mid-1980s, Makovsky & Co., an independent public and investor relations consulting firm, in New York City, has been monitoring client relationships by asking account managers for written feedback. But in 1992, founder Ken Makovsky started asking his customers for their input, too.

Makovsky sends small clients a detailed questionnaire once a year; large, complex accounts are surveyed semiannually. Team leaders **make follow-up phone calls** to their 50-odd clients to encourage them to complete the questionnaires. Makovsky estimates that 80% return the surveys.

The process has elicited candid feedback and revelations from customers. One client, for example, had worked with Makovsky & Co. for five years and then coldly invited the agency to rebid on the expired contract. Makovsky didn't get the bid, but he called the client—only to discover that the president had never liked the account manager.

The survey has also cleared up other misunderstandings. One international client, which was habitually late paying its bills, needed to have the invoice routed through its U.S. division. Suddenly, a 90-day billing cycle turned into 30.

Makovsky & Co. has realized an improved client-retention rate—up 22% from prereview years. Better yet, 20% of the company's $6.5 million in net revenue now comes from client referrals.

Who Was That Masked Shopper?

When you have one location, quality control is simple. But as a company grows, it's hard to keep tabs on everything. The founders of the Ruby's chain of restaurants use mystery shoppers—individuals hired to pose as customers who report on how they were treated. Here are some tips for **using mystery shoppers effectively**.

- *Think first.* Fashion your questionnaire to track the qualities of service that are important to your company.

- *Be consistent.* A key to making the program work is having a mystery shopper visit on a regular basis. For Ruby's, that means calling on each of its seven restaurants at least once a month. At $30 a visit, the program costs Ruby's about $200 a month, plus the price of the meal.

- *Push hot buttons.* You can use the shoppers to reinforce a particular program, such as suggestive selling. Asking a customer if she wants orange juice with her breakfast can boost the average check. In Ruby's mystery-shopper survey, suggestive-selling questions carry extra weight.

- *Make sure everybody has the answers.* The idea behind the surveys is to reward the staff and improve customer service. Tell all employees what's on the survey and which questions are most important.

144 IDEA

Instant Gratification

At some point, haven't we all answered a customer-service survey, only to experience little or no change in service? Pattie Paddy, president and CEO of Kwik Kopy Corp., uses what she finds out from her surveys of a demanding bunch of customers: her franchise owners.

According to Paddy, "Every month, our franchise services representatives (currently eight) call all of our domestic centers (more than 550) and make two requests: 'Give me one thing to do for you,' and 'Please rate us on a scale of 1 to 10'." Callers make sure that the request is acted upon. They also pass along any industry and corporate news to the franchise owner. "Every morning we meet to talk about the previous day's calls," says Paddy. "We talk about whether we can or need to do more for an owner, we can spot market and system trends, and we discuss specific issues that may arise."

Kwik Kopy finds that **pairing staff with franchise owners** gives customer service a personal and more effective touch. "We really get to know our customers and, hopefully, anticipate some of their needs to help us act quickly," Paddy says.

145
IDEA

First-Date Proposal

What would you pay for a tactic that gets new customers into your store, provides an unbiased report on your company's service, and brings you lots of new ideas? Gary Cino, CEO of the 98¢ Clearance Centers chain, based in North Highland, Calif., thought it was worth $5.

When Cino met someone who had never set foot in one of his 60 retail stores, which gross almost $400 million annually, he handed the prospect a retail-value booklet, a self-addressed stamped envelope, and a questionnaire with a dozen queries. The **first-timers were asked to rate the store's appearance and products**, note the friendliness of the staff, and add any comments or suggestions. Customers were also asked to attach copies of their cash-register receipts.

Cino and his executives passed out some 500 packets a year, which amounted to a $2,500 cash expense. But approximately 85% of the shoppers returned the survey within 90 days. The attached receipts showed that most of the new customers spent considerably more than $5. The feedback was worth even more. "It let our employees know that at any time, any customer could report back to management," said Cino. As for changes, he arranged an 800-number phone response system and started distributing gift packets to teachers, who could reward students with "Outstanding Achiever Award" coupons redeemable at Cino's shops.

146
IDEA

Get to the Root

We always had customer-complaint forms. You'd fill 'em out, sign 'em, and send 'em to somebody. But what did we learn from them? They were simply filed away," says Dave Franceschi, quality-support manager of Granite Rock, a supplier of building and construction materials, based in Watsonville, Calif. "The result was that we had no way of keeping the problem from happening again."

Today, every complaint generates a **product-service-discrepancy (PSD) report**, a copy of which lands on Franceschi's desk. Over time, he can chart exactly where problems lie and how much each one costs the company.

The critical line on the PSD reports is the one marked "root-cause analysis." In the past, a bad batch of asphalt might be ascribed to "dirty rock," a term that refers to an aggregate with too many fine particles. Today, Franceschi won't accept a PSD unless it offers a true explanation, such as "faulty screen at the quarry." The explanation alone usually shows what must be done to correct the problem.

"No great marketing decisions have ever been made on quantitative data."

JOHN SCULLEY
former CEO of Apple Computer
(*The Manager's Book of Quotations*
by Lewis D. Eigen and Jonathan P. Siegel,
AMACOM, 1989)

Where'd We Go Wrong?

Most company owners hate to hear harsh words about their "babies." To avoid that discomfort, Bob Ottley, president of One Step Tree and Lawn Care, in North Chili, N.Y., used an independent consulting firm to conduct One Step's first telephone survey. The firm called current customers as well as those who had canceled its service. The results were sobering: A full 32%—or 719 of 2,250 customers—had defected, and many wouldn't say why.

Now One Step persistently keeps track of its customer list, and Ottley **acts on the weekly "cancels" report**. He's halved the attrition rate and knows why customers failed to renew. In the first half of 1994, for example, 19% of nonrenewers had moved, 16% decided to maintain their lawns themselves, 12% could no longer afford the service, and 8% opted for a cheaper competitor. Among the rest, only 4% gave no explanation. After that first poll, One Step's revenues grew to $1.6 million in 1996.

148
IDEA

Four-Star Staff Schooling

When a cook for Chef Allen's sampled a competitor's fare, he was dismayed to find elegant food being served on cold plates. It ruined the meal, the cook reported at a staff meeting. "He thought more about warming up plates after that," says Allen Susser, owner of the $3-million restaurant, in North Miami Beach, Fla.

The cook is not the only employee with a nose for customer-service details, thanks to a program his boss started a few years ago. Susser's program, called "Chow Now," boils down to **sensitivity training**. The owner wanted his servers and cooks to experience fine dining firsthand. Great idea, said the staff, but it's not in our budget. So Susser began giving selected employees $50 each to dine at any restaurant with cuisine similar to that of Chef Allen's. Employees return with brief written and oral reports on what they learned.

Nearly all 30 staffers have participated, at a rate of two or three feedback sessions a month. Susser's return is palatable: Chef Allen's consistently receives rave reviews for food and service, and employee turnover is low.

Accentuate the Negative

In customer-service circles, no news is bad news. Ruppert Landscape, located in Ashton, Md., gets a respectable 60% return on its twice-a-year customer-satisfaction surveys. Most of the 750 accounts give the company high marks. But it's the 40% who don't respond that cause management worry.

"We assume the worst," says Chris Davitt, vice-president of the company. "Those customers could be about to leave, and we need to reach them. We send out a follow-up letter that yields another 20%." A manager visits or phones the remaining 20%, as well as clients who gave Ruppert a negative report. **Massaging discontented and unresponsive customers** is time-consuming, but it pays off in increasingly larger renewal contracts and fewer bad debts.

Focus on a Few

When daily customer interactions can number in the hundreds, try a **focused approach to quality control**.

Team One Plastics, in Albion, Mich., involves employee teams with customer contacts. "We often work with a dozen key people at a customer site of 100 or more employees. When problems occur, their 12 can talk to our 12," says cofounder Craig Carrel. "How we all interact is part of the give-and-take of building a relationship."

Classy Chassis, a car-wash chain, based in Biloxi, Miss., balances its need for speed with "exit people" who check quality before customers drive off. And customers of special detailing services—such as hand waxing—are asked to rate performance. "We see 300 to 400 cars a day, so we focus on 10 to 25 at each of our sites," says owner Tom Wall. Customers who fill out a survey get 50% off their next wash. Demand for detailing work, a profit maker, has grown considerably.

How Do You Love Us?

Faced with chronically low response rates, many small businesses have to be creative and proactive when soliciting customer feedback.

Customer-comment cards are often served up with dessert, but Chef Allen's, a North Miami Beach, Fla., restaurant, tops them off with a phone call. "For parties of eight or more, we **call the host of the party the next day** to make sure it went well," says owner Allen Susser. "We know that with a big party we can lose control of what happens. Hosts may be too diplomatic to complain in front of others, but they tend to be important customers who spend a lot of money."

Carneiro, Chumney & Co., a San Antonio accounting firm, **encloses a short questionnaire with each invoice**. It saves stamps, but there's another reason for doing it. "When a customer pays the bill, it's the ultimate evaluation," says managing partner Bob McAdams. "It's one more snapshot of how we're doing." Of those who return the card, only 1% give Carneiro less than a 4.2 rating on a scale of one to five.

The Score on Sports Sponsorship

Shortly after starting up in 1979, $15-million Frozfruit, based in Los Angeles, began **sponsoring road races and other sporting events** to introduce its frozen-fruit bars and get feedback on products in the lab. "It's the best way to get close to our target customers—health-conscious adults," said president Charlie O'Brien. He sent his product and reps to more than 100 events a year nationwide. Race participants sampled the fruit bars, picked up coupons, T-shirts, and hats, and walked by a table stacked with short product surveys—which received a 50% response rate.

Coupon redemption usually jumped after race events, but the real payoff was the market research. When survey results suggested a new flavor was too tart or too sweet, Frozfruit tweaked it before sending the bars to store shelves. The feedback also helped the company to determine pricing and sell distributors on new products.

The cost? About $100,000 a year. O'Brien said he considered the cost a long-term investment because it goes toward building distributor and customer relations. He targeted mostly small events at which Frozfruit gained more exposure, and the sponsorship fees were low.

"The customers you lose hold the information you need to succeed."

FREDERICK F. REICHHELD
director of Bain & Company, in Boston,
and author of *The Loyalty Effect*
(Harvard Business School Press, 1996)

153
IDEA

One Door Closes, Another One Opens

T&K Roofing Co., a contractor, in Ely, Iowa, had sprung a leak. Profit margins had dwindled from 5% to 1% on sales of $2.5 million. To patch things up, Kurt Tjelmeland, T&K's vice-president, designed the **Lost-Job Survey, which asked would-be customers why they rejected his company's bid**.

Half of the survey questions were designed to determine how T&K was being represented in the field. Answers to other questions revealed why competitors were nipping away at T&K's 68% market share.

Often the questionnaire kept alive a relationship that might otherwise have ended. When prospects returned forms that told of a particularly harrowing experience with T&K, they received a call from Tjelmeland and were sent a gift certificate for dinner.

The strategy paid off: The phone call and free dinner ended the relationship on an upbeat note, and several companies asked T&K to submit bids for other projects. Since it began using the Lost-Job Survey, the company nearly doubled its sales to $6 million, even though eight new competitors had entered the market.

The Check's in the Mail

Slow payers can often provide valuable information about financial or other glitches within your organization. Maybe your customers aren't paying on time because you shipped something they didn't order, or you sent the wrong quantity and the customer is angry. Or, perhaps your company sent an invoice before it shipped the product, and the customer filed it away, forgetting all about it. Maybe your sales staffers made special deals with customers about delivery dates or other conditions—but then forgot to inform the rest of your organization.

Jim Shaw, owner and president of Shaw Resources, a Cupertino, Calif., company that advises clients on how to improve management systems, suggests **courting slow payers with a willingness to fix what's wrong**. "Approach the call with a respectful, cordial demeanor, starting with the assumption that the client is honest, wants to pay you, and must have a reason for delay," says Shaw. After that, it's up to your company to resolve the problem quickly. "If the customer fails to pay you promptly at that point, then—and only then—is it time to ask yourself if you've got a problem customer."

IDEA

Doing It Their Way

Sixty percent of all the printing done in America is either screwed up or late," says Tom Carns, owner of PDQ, a Las Vegas-based printing company. So, Carns sees to it that his company does what it can to **ensure customers get their way—and on time**. Here are some of his strategies.

With every job, Carns sends a survey dubbed *Two Sides to Every Story*, explaining to customers that PDQ tries to do things right and on time. The form has a blank side, which it asks customers to use to tell their side of the story.

Every December PDQ schedules "defense-defense" sales calls. "We go out in person to our 150 largest customers, thank them for their business, and ask how we can improve things," says Carns. "We also ask, 'What kind of printing are you buying elsewhere that you're not getting from us?'" When "continuous forms" kept cropping up as the answer, PDQ decided to produce them. In 1996, PDQ sold continuous forms to 35% of its commercial accounts, boosting total sales.

Know Thy Customers

Why is it, Ford R. Myers asked himself, that my company can deliver jobs of equal quality to two clients, and one thinks we're great while the other never wants to deal with us again?

Myers concluded that Ford Myers & Co., located in Haverford, Pa., could better serve its clients by tailoring the company's operating style to their individual expectations. Now he **culls a customer profile from a one-page list of questions** that he now asks all clients. Getting the information for the profile takes Myers only about 15 minutes per customer. He briefs the staff on every new client and staples the typed profile to the job folder so everyone involved can easily refer to it.

The questions try to ascertain procedural ground rules: On the project's satisfactory completion, will you require a detailed itemization of costs, or will our invoice be adequate? And they attempt to set priorities: Which is of paramount importance to your company—scheduling and budget, or innovation and creativity?

Afterward, Myers often likes to chat informally with the client. When asked which is more important, maximum quality or staying within budget, many clients will say both, but Myers's probing often reveals a distinct preference for one or the other. "I believe every client has one real primary concern," says Myers.

157
IDEA

A Family Affair

The person who writes the check may not be your only customer. One family member may appear to be the driving force in a purchase, but that person may turn out not to be the decision maker or primary user. "Customer satisfaction is a function of everyone who uses the product, so we try to **involve all family members in the purchase process**," says Doug Steimle, CEO of California Pools and Spas, a $60-million company, headquartered in West Covina, Calif.

It's not unusual to discover that different family members envision different pools—an aesthetically pleasing design, a lap lane for exercise, a diving board, or a slide. Sales reps are instructed to inquire about everyone's needs. Do you need handrails and a gradual entry area for grandparents? Do you want a large deck for social gatherings?

"We make a point of interviewing as many family members as possible," says Steimle. "If we can't talk to them directly, we ask the person we're dealing with to specifically consider their needs. This encourages the buyer to seek the opinions of others before the next meeting. Kids should be involved too. We provide a coloring book to educate kids on the pool-building process. They can entertain themselves but still be present to add their views."

By getting everyone involved in the design process, the company shows its customers that it wants to satisfy their needs, instead of just putting a product in their backyards. "Involving everyone is good for customer satisfaction, and it's good for sales," Steimle notes.

Inside Inspiration

Employees know what they need most to serve customers best," says Patty Remen, corporate relations manager for The Davis Companies. The $47-million staffing and human-resources management company, in Marlborough, Mass., uses a two-stage process to tap the insights of its 1,500 employees.

In the first stage, suggestions for improvement are requested in the comment section of **periodic employee surveys**. Twice a year, a tear-off page is added to employee time cards, requesting comments: "How can we better serve you, and how can you better serve our customers?" Employees have generated ideas such as the introduction of client handbooks, improved communication between divisions serving the same client, phone training for all employees, and increased staffing at the reception desk.

In the second stage, employees are asked to rate the importance of 100 or more ideas generated in the first stage. "Employees are there on the job, not management," notes Remen, "so they have the clearest idea of which improvements are needed most to serve customers. Their ideas and insights are central in our quality efforts."

The surveys have definitely improved Davis's services. One employee suggested more in-depth training for an assembly position at a manufacturing client company, so Davis designed a customized, on-site training program for staff in that position. "The client was so impressed with the results, it asked us to train its employees as well," says Remen. "Something that started as a way to improve service to our client became a revenue generator for us."

Well, What Did You Expect?

Satisfaction surveys often ask customers whether their expectations were met. A surprising number of dissatisfied customers report that their expectations *were* met. What are these customers telling you? To find out, Applied Intelligence Group (AIG), a 125-person computer consulting firm, in Edmond, Okla., asked them.

Some customers felt that their central expectations were met, but that they hadn't anticipated negative impacts of the project. Other customers changed their specifications after the contract was signed, and the company's effort to accommodate these changes led to increased costs, delayed deadlines, or additional customer effort.

To learn how to help future customers anticipate project contingencies, the company's **satisfaction survey now contains more detailed questions about expectations**. Did customers underestimate the extent to which their employees would be involved in the project? Did changes in the project result in higher costs, delays, or extra work for the customer's staff? The company uses the information to educate future customers about the likelihood of changing expectations and the level of their involvement in projects. It then tracks the effectiveness of the company's education efforts.

By asking the right questions, says John Duck, vice-president of finance, AIG has learned how changing expectations affect customer satisfaction and how to manage those expectations. As a result, AIG has increased customer satisfaction to the point where 80% of revenue comes from repeat business, and an additional 10% of sales are traceable to referrals from satisfied customers.

Yes, We Do Alterations

Three years ago, when Katherine Barchetti of K. Barchetti Shops, in Pittsburgh, wrote letters to 3,000 people asking why they no longer shopped at her clothing and shoe stores, 290 people wrote back. Although it took her a year and a half to reply to each person, she quickly responded to the feedback by saying good-bye to an unfriendly manager and modifying her prices.

"If you're not using the data you're collecting, don't ask for it," Barchetti advises. For the past 30 years she has been gathering client information that helps her squeeze out a profitable $3 million in annual revenues from two tiny shops.

In the mid-'80s, Barchetti's late husband developed a software package to integrate sales records and customer buying patterns that Katherine had culled throughout the '60s, '70s, and '80s. He pumped 20 years of hand-written customer information into the database, and her staff **analyzed the data to improve her offerings**. Paying attention to that information has meant an average 8% increase in gross profits per year for the last seven years, faster inventory turnover, and more sharply focused direct-mail campaigns. A recent mailer to 5,000 top-spending customers brought in 181 shoppers, who purchased $90,000 worth of merchandise in one week—representing a 96% increase in total sales over the same week the previous year.

161
IDEA

Predictable Adventures

What sets Adventure Travel apart from its competition is an exquisite sensitivity to customer needs, say owners Alan and Roger Hale. To stay attuned to its clients, the Birmingham, Ala., agency **monitors its customer service** in various ways:

- Adventure Travel's associates consult with travel arrangers, managers, and travelers to chart client needs for the upcoming year; to review purchasing trends, reporting techniques, and data collected; to discuss updates to a traveler's profile; and to help design on-site partnership seminars that make travel simpler and easier.
- The agency issues postage-paid, self-addressed quick-response surveys with every airline ticket (on alternate months) to garner invaluable input from 7,500 travelers. Adventure Travel also contacts 200 randomly selected clients to discuss responses to customer-satisfaction questionnaires. Weaknesses and suggestions for improvement are addressed in semiannual companywide meetings and quarterly manager meetings.
- An outside consultant audits the agency's systems throughout the year. A mystery caller places a call to each employee and rates his or her knowledge, level of courtesy, desire to please, and customer-service spirit. The company responds to complaints within 24 hours, initially with the traveler, then with the agent. After attempting to solve the problem, policies are changed to prevent a recurrence.

Does it fly? You bet! Adventure Travel has more than doubled its staff in seven years, operating 11 offices in Alabama, Georgia, and Florida. The company currently generates approximately $75 million in revenues annually, placing it among the top 100 travel agencies in the country.

162
IDEA

Focus Lens on Focus Groups

Most people are aware of customer focus groups, in which customers are brought together and asked by a professional facilitator their opinions regarding a product or service. In initial business-to-business satisfaction focus groups, key account contacts are usually asked a number of pointed questions about their expectations and how well the supplier is meeting them.

Joseph P. Sperry, a consultant and a partner with S4 Consulting, based in Powell, Ohio, suggests taking the customer-service survey a step further. **Video focus groups** can enable a company to get systematic customer expectation data and improve training and performance.

Because the focus groups are videotaped, an edited record of customer responses will be available for uses that are limited only by the firm's creativity. Such tapes can work to:

- Tighten and align the questions on satisfaction surveys
- Bring the "voice of the customer" directly to internal training programs
- Help determine which internal delivery systems fall short of customer expectations
- Develop quicker employee buy-in for any process or system-improvement effort.

Face-to-Face Feedback

There's no substitute for getting together with customers to discuss how you can best meet their needs. **Inviting customers for breakfast or lunch** can help increase feedback.

When Deck House, located in Acton, Mass., was wrestling with changes in the design and marketing of its post-and-beam house kits, it invited customers to attend a design session. "We had some specific things we wanted to look at during that meeting, and we brought customers in to see what they thought," says Michael Harris, Deck House president and CEO.

The results helped the company see ways it could better distinguish itself from the competition. "It was very useful," says Harris. "We got information on color, style, process, and price."

Visiting your customers for no reason other than to ask them about your company's performance can also pay big dividends. Make an appointment in advance, make it clear that you don't want to sell them anything, and tell them you are looking for some ideas to help serve them better.

"Because its purpose is to create
a customer, the business
enterprise has two—and only
these two—basic functions:
marketing and innovation.
Marketing and innovation
produce results;
all the rest are 'costs.' "

PETER F. DRUCKER
management guru and author of *People and Performance*
(Harper & Row, 1977)

164
IDEA

Board of Education

The key to outstanding customer service is to find out what customers want and then give it to them. The best way to do that, contends Gary Nelson, is to form a **customer advisory board** to help you see your customer's point of view.

Nelson runs Arrowhead Nursery, a $2-million garden center, located in Wayland, Mass. His nearest competitor is only a half mile away. Rather than just talking to walk-ins, Nelson invites between five to seven customers, who vary in income and in their degree of happiness with his business, to sit for a year on an advisory board. The board members meet three times a year to tell Nelson whether they liked new displays, whether new products proved to be of high quality, and whether employees were helpful and courteous. Nelson then presents his upcoming plans and asks for critiques. Once board members see some of their ideas implemented, Nelson says, they get all fired up.

Nelson asks his staff to nominate customers as potential board members. Once a year he asks nominees to serve as advisers. Nelson takes board members to a different restaurant for each of the three lunchtime meetings, gives them a $50 gift certificate, and tries to get the local paper to list their names when they are appointed. "You don't have to make a big deal over it," Nelson says. "Just show a little appreciation."

Advocate for the Customer

Busy managers often put off maintenance duties until equipment breaks down or the supply closet is empty. Not so for customers of Super Wash, a company based in Morrisson, Ill., that builds self-service car washes. Super Wash customers get quarterly reminders from the company's **customer advocate, whose job is to nip potential service crises in the bud** and keep customer relations positive rather than adversarial.

Four times a year, the 450 owners and operators of Super Wash car washes receive a phone call from a proactive service representative. The rep finds out whether their equipment has been functioning properly, what glitches they have encountered in receiving supplies or parts from the company, or whether they need any help preparing for a big event. Summaries of the conversations are then handed over directly to Bob and Mary Black, cofounders and chiefs of the company, as a way for them to monitor the quality of service customers are receiving.

"We depend upon the quality of our service and referrals to sell new car washes," says Mary Black, who notes that because of the proactive service customers receive, the company employs just one salesperson on staff and "there is no wining and dining here." Black says the customer advocate position more than pays for itself.

"What's the danger of giving away too much? Are you worried about having an oversatisfied customer? That's not much of a worry. You can forget about an oversatisfied customer, but an unsatisfied customer is one of the most expensive problems you can have."

JAN CARLZON
former CEO of Scandinavian Airlines System (SAS),
in Stockholm, Sweden, and author of *Moments of Truth*
(Ballinger Publishing, 1987)

Question Priority

Some customers hate to feel rushed and want lots of time with the service provider. How can you tell which customers want speedy service and which prefer a leisurely pace? Ask them!

That is just what optometrist Dr. Henry Samson does in his New Haven, Conn., practice. When medical histories are collected at the beginning of the visit, **patients are asked about their priorities**. Questions asked include: Are you in a hurry? Do you want comprehensive information today, or should the doctor focus on the most important points to accommodate a busy schedule? Patients appreciate having their preferences taken into account, and the doctor ends up spending the right amount of time with each individual.

Calculating Your Worth to Customers

The more customers can quantify the return on their investment, the happier they are. When companies invest in employee education, they want to know that employees are applying their newly learned skills. According to Ann Angel, president of a computer-training firm, in Winston-Salem, N.C., you can strengthen your customer relationships if you **help clients quantify the value they get from your services**.

One month after a training session, Angel's Technologies Training of the Triad (TTT) surveys trainees to find out what percentage use the specific computer skills taught in the class. A follow-up survey requires more effort than the warm and fuzzy questions typically asked at the end of a class, such as "Did you like the instructor?"

Angel says, "The extra effort of the follow-up survey is definitely worthwhile." TTT trainers use the feedback to improve future classes. Corporate training managers use the positive results as ammunition to justify future training expenditures. And, TTT differentiates itself from the competition by its willingness to help customers calculate the value of the service.

How are things going for the firm? TTT has a client roster of 350 and a retention rate just under 100%, after 10 years in business.

168
IDEA

Nothing Beats Instant Delivery

Like most sophisticated manufacturers, Interconnect Devices International (IDI), an industry leader in spring contact probes, follows the principles of just-in-time manufacturing. But sometimes schedule sharing, electronic data interchange, overnight delivery, and the like just aren't good enough. This Kansas City, Kans., manufacturer found itself at a disadvantage against competitors on the East and West Coasts that could provide same-day delivery to coastal customers.

IDI overcame the problem with a **consignment stock program** for its high-volume customers. IDI stores inventory at the customer's location in a locked storage cabinet. The customer withdraws precoded bags and checks off the item on a listing sheet. Once a week the customer faxes the inventory record to IDI, an invoice is issued, and stock is replenished.

"Customers receive same-second delivery and are guaranteed that needed parts are in stock," says Kelly Robb, IDI's inside sales supervisor. To minimize the effect on inventory levels, the dedicated stock is offered only on fast, continuously moving items. Total inventory is reduced by focusing on cutting back slow-moving and obsolete stock. For customers who do not have the time or resources to self-manage consignment stock, IDI offers a safety stock program. Inventory is stored in a separate location for each customer and shipped upon request.

"Customers appreciate the fact that we take a risk," says Robb. "This has allowed us to become the exclusive supplier to large players in the industry and thus increase stock turns." Another benefit of the consignment stock program is that IDI is able to learn more about customer needs by getting product feedback directly from the end-user.

There's Butter in the Batter

To support strong sales of its frozen batter, Main Street Gourmet, an $8-million company, based in Cuyahoga Falls, Ohio, makes it easy for retailers to bake and market its products by providing professional nonstick pans, portion-control scoops, and baking-pan spray at cost.

Main Street Gourmet uses its purchasing power to help retailers with capital expenses associated with preparation, storage, and selling, as well as the convenience of **"one-stop-shopping" without charging a profit on the equipment**. This particularly helps start-up customers, says Chris Roman, director of sales. The company also supplies display cases, at cost, to ensure that muffins will be attractively displayed, while maximizing shelf-life. Merchandising materials are offered free. "Customers recognize that we offer these supplies as a service and are grateful—it helps build customer loyalty, and we sell more of our frozen batter," says Roman. Indeed, sales have increased an average of 45% per year since 1990.

Vaccination Against Viruses

Extra customer service doesn't have to be expensive. San Diego-based GERS Retail Systems designed its Web page to **give customers the option of downloading antivirus software**. Once the antivirus program is installed, customers can download how-to documents or answers to frequently asked questions—without fear of importing a virus that could impede the use of software applications or damage existing files.

GERS also uses its Web page to provide online support and services, including networking opportunities. "We encourage customers to share ideas with each other on our secured bulletin board," says Comley. "It's a great way for customers to find solutions to common problems."

"The antivirus software developer likes to get its name out, so it gave us permission to include this program for free," says Tess Comley, manager of corporate standards for the developer of system solutions for retailers. "Several of our 300 customers have written to say it's a great idea. Customers appreciate that we're thinking of ways to protect them from system downtime caused by a virus. It's simple to do, and it makes us look good."

171
IDEA

Help Your Customers Network

Customers can learn from each other when you bring them together with user conferences, seminars, and Internet bulletin boards. If you encourage them to meet in your presence, you build relationships that can help build future business for you.

This personal approach to one-on-one introductions is recommended by Shirley Singleton, president and CEO of Edgewater Technology, located in Wakefield, Mass. Singleton arranges about a dozen **field trips** per year that connect two customers of her $12-million custom software-solutions development company. She looks for win-win situations in which both customers benefit. Once, she introduced a client seeking to outsource phone order taking with another who provided that service. She also brought together two insurance companies that wanted to learn about each other's sales vehicles.

The field trips allow customers to observe business operations that offer a solution to their own problems. "Customers like to see battle scars first-hand—what went wrong and how problems were solved," says Singleton, "rather than a polished slide show from a consultant."

Cross-customer introductions don't necessarily mean short-term business for Edgewater. "We help customers build relationships with partners, and that builds our relationships with them," says Singleton. "Our credibility increases, and long-term business results when educated customers reengineer their businesses."

"Today customers want more.
They want more information
about the products they buy, more
input into the product itself,
and more support after
the sale…The more you can get
them involved in the process of
customizing the product and the
selling process to meet their
particular needs, the more likely
that you will get the sale."

LEN KEELER
author of *Cybermarketing*
(AMACOM, 1995)

Simplified Shopping

Are you complicating your customers' lives by offering too many choices? Take note of the **custom catalogs** produced by ISE Office Plus, a Bronx, N.Y., office-supply dealer. ISE uses past buying patterns and customer input to produce for each customer a customized minicatalog containing several hundred frequently purchased items. Buyers no longer have to waste time wading through a 25,000-item volume to find the blue pens they usually order.

Cost-conscious customers love the custom catalog. The supplies are specially priced, and purchase selection is limited to approved items—no more expensive neon sticky notes or gold paper clips to tempt them. As an added service, ISE prints the customer's purchasing procedures in the catalog. New employees at these companies find this all-in-one instruction manual a useful tool.

Commercially, the catalogs have been a big success. "Custom catalog sales account for over 50% of our business," says Bill Rountry, director of sales at ISE. "The catalog cements our relationship with the buyer—we've never lost a custom-catalog customer."

Make Your Customer a Winner

Out-of-the-box thinking comes naturally to David Diederich, president of Pactech, a $4.5-million company, located in Rochester, N.Y., that designs and manufactures flexible packaging. Diederich looked at the relationships his company was building with his customers and thought of a great way to promote both his customers and his design expertise in one neat package.

Pactech designers and technical staff work closely with a customer's in-house engineering team to develop packaging products. Some of these products have the potential to win industry awards for design. Diederich's idea: **enter design competitions in the customer's name**, not Pactech's, to win recognition for the customer's in-house engineering team. Pactech pays contest entrance fees, coordinates the submission of supporting documents, and sometimes pays for winners to attend the award ceremonies.

The customer's advertising department uses the award for publicity, and the winner gets recognition that can lead to promotion. But Pactech's role does not go unnoticed. The competition process enhances Pactech's profile with the winning company, and Diederich credits its success with increased sales. After winning an award, annual sales for one product went from $10,000 to $1.3 million.

Family Fun Wins Fans

Want to delight customers? **Entertain their kids**. If you can supply a service that children enjoy and that solves a parental problem, you'll be a big hit.

- *Do something fun.* Holiday Inn Capitol at the Smithsonian, a 280-employee hotel, located in Washington D.C., lets kids under eight years old opt for a sleeping bag instead of a rollaway bed. "Kids just love it. They view it as an adventure," says the hotel's general manager Dean Wilhelm. This option also makes the stay easier for mom and dad, and, as an added bonus, less space is taken up by a cot in their room. The housekeepers love it, too, notes Wilhelm, because it means less clean-up for them.

- *Offer free tickets for kids.* The Portland String Quartet wanted its afternoon concerts to be enjoyable for parents, but realized some adults were uncertain about spending money on tickets for their kids. As a pitch, the Portland, Maine, chamber music group now invites children under 21 to attend concerts free of charge. Families can enjoy their afternoons together, and the Quartet has an opportunity to cultivate a new generation of consumers.

Go for the Long Haul

Sound advice is one of the services customers seek when they hire a professional. That advice can be hard to give when it means lower revenues for the service provider. Nonetheless, Paul Arpin Van Lines, located in West Warwick, R.I., is committed to **looking after the customer's interests—even if it's at the company's expense**. According to John Leistritz, vice president of marketing, helping customers avoid unnecessary expense and stress generates repeat and referral business that leads to long-term profitability.

What's Arpin's suggestion to customers? Move fewer items. The van line's moving guide warns that one of the biggest mistakes people make is to take everything they own. The company advises people to be "ruthless" about selling or donating every questionable item—strong advice from a company that gets paid to move stuff.

Arpin's advice has paid off by fueling long-term revenue growth—a $25-million increase in one year. Leistritz says customers often thank the company for convincing them to leave belongings such as firewood and junk cars, because the cost of moving them exceeds their replacement cost. A less costly (and less stressful) move for clients means reputation, referrals, and long-term profits for the van line.

Keep Your Head Out of the Sand

CM Trailers, in Madill, Okla., makes all types of animal trailers, including one for ostriches. "Going to an extreme has been our call to glory," says Ron Jackson, founder and CEO. And, Jackson notes, all customers have good ideas about what they want—no matter how strange they sound on first mention.

Jackson's biggest challenge is persuading short-sighted dealers to **welcome unusual requests from potential customers**. "Dealers shouldn't tell their customers they're out of touch with reality, because the customers will find someone else who'll listen. When you educate yourself, you educate your customer." He also advocates team sales. The dealer should be proud to say, "This is what we all came up with—salesperson, manufacturer, and customer." Jackson's approach is working: Last year, CM Trailers' collaborative approach reaped $17 million in sales.

177
IDEA

Ideas You Can Deliver

Bill Duggan, managing partner of Videoport, a video rental store, in Portland, Maine, knows that personalized service and creativity are required to compete against large chains. For inspiration on new services, Duggan looks to noncompeting businesses. "By **taking service ideas from other industries**, we've increased rentals, reached new niche markets, and have improved customer satisfaction," says Duggan.

If pizza can be delivered, why can't videos? Videoport now delivers videos seven nights a week. Delivery accounts for 10% of movie rentals, and some customers have all of their rentals delivered.

Another old, but new-to-the-video-business, idea is credit. Similar to bartenders running a tab for customers, the system spares patrons the hassle of continually rummaging for change or writing checks. "Our frequent renters love the system," says Duggan.

"A certain percentage of customers default," says Duggan, "but we more than make up for it in increased sales per customer. People don't limit themselves to what they have in their pocket. Our average number of rental copies per person is higher than the industry average."

Videoport has been voted "best video store" four years in a row in the local newspaper's annual survey, and it dominates video rentals in the local market. Success has come, in part, from its ability to identify services that customers value.

178
IDEA

Keep Customers in the Know to Grow

We want our clients to understand the market and how to get ahead," says Victoria Manning, marketing analyst for John Hewitt and Associates (JHA), a risk management and consulting firm, in Portland, Maine. "**If clients need information to grow, we'll get it for them**, free of charge, so we can grow with them."

Twice a year, JHA gathers sales information on every firm in the disability market and distributes the results to both customers and noncustomers. Companies use the information to benchmark how well they're doing against the competition and to tout their industry ranking in their promotional materials. "The survey generates media attention," says Manning, "and positions our firm as an expert in the field. New clients often cite the research as the reason for seeking us out."

JHA provides another client service: a broker survey. Clients submit the names of 1,000 independent brokers who sell their insurance products. The brokers are surveyed to find out how the clients can better serve them. "Clients say this is exactly what they need," says Manning. "It helps them design and market new products."

JHA also keeps its clients informed on industry trends, recent court decisions, and new products introduced by competitors. "Providing market research differentiates us from the competition," says Manning. "We attract new customers and keep our current ones—our retention rate is 90%. The growth of the long-term disability market, due in part to our research efforts, is good for our customers and good for us."

Pearls of Wisdom

There is no secret formula for success," says Ellen Daigle, president of Ellen's Silkscreening & Imprinted Promotional Products, a South Pasadena, Calif., company with $1.5 million in revenues. This award-winning entrepreneur credits her success to hard work and a company-wide dedication to getting the job done right. If you want to run a business, she says, **don't have problems. Either anticipate and prevent them, or approach them as a challenge**. Here's how Daigle does it.

1) Great service and on-time delivery are the best advertising tools you have. If something is wrong, make it right. Charge the expense to advertising instead of viewing it as a loss.

2) If you need to make a product substitution or other change, consult your customer beforehand, not after the fact. Most customers could care less when asked. If you make the decision for them, it raises all their suspicions.

3) Deliver on time. Daigle, who has never missed a delivery, sets an internal deadline two days earlier than the date promised.

4) People skills are imperative for you and your employees. The need to be right is not as important as the ability to compromise.

5) Coach and train your staff. Invest in employees by coaching them and sending them to training classes. They'll serve the company and the customers better.

6) Reread your procedures—you probably have some good ideas that you've forgotten.

We Do the Difficult

What would you do if asked to remove a snake from a conference room or perform a service beyond the terms of your contract? You'll get the job done if you're Dave Pasek, president of Service Performance Corp., a janitorial company, in San Jose, Calif. "We **make every effort to say yes to every customer**, in every situation, every day," says Pasek. "It's our 'difficult yes' policy. We only turn down requests that are immoral, illegal, or unsafe."

The majority of requests are for unscheduled, last-minute service. Pasek and his 1,000 employees do what it takes—they find the staff, rent the equipment, have the account manager work alongside the custodian. Some requests fall outside the range of custodial work. The company has helped clients put together budgets and has worked with other vendors to supply forklift operators and painting services.

Sounds easy? It's not. "This isn't something you just roll out," asserts Pasek. "Everyone in the firm has to understand customer service and its importance. Employees need to be empowered to act without seeking permission. They need to know that management will back them up." The "difficult yes" policy is part of employee training. It is reinforced at biweekly management meetings and weekly supervisor meetings that end with five minutes for sharing "difficult yes" examples.

Since 1993, sales have increased fivefold, and the company's customer retention rate is 96%.

From Small Screen to Big Screen

Success in a retail business may mean long lines for impatient customers. When wait times can't be reduced, the situation can still be improved by **adding value to the wait**.

Flagship Cinemas, in Falmouth, Maine, has accomplished this by adding a bank of television sets along the wall where lines form. The screens are used to show short previews of coming attractions. General manager Andrew Poore says that on busy nights—particularly on weekends—the previews make the lines more manageable. "You look out in the lobby, and everyone is watching the clips," he notes. "Customers are surprised at how quickly the time passes. They hardly realize they're in a line."

The clips, which are changed about once a month, are an additional expense for the cinema, but the results are worth it. "Customers appreciate being entertained—after all, that's why they're here," says Poore. "It makes the whole experience more enjoyable."

Reflect on Diversity

As businesses expand domestically and internationally, they are likely to encounter a customer base of increasing cultural diversity. By **hiring a heterogeneous workforce**, a company shows respect for the diversity of its customers, and it may increase the extent to which customers identify with employees.

The Support Center for Nonprofit Management, a San Francisco resource center for administrators of nonprofit organizations, makes a point of maintaining a staff and a board of directors that mirror its customer base in terms of ethnicity, gender, and other demographics. The result is that each subpopulation is included in the company's decision-making processes.

"We feel that a staff and board of directors that represent the diversity of our clients will be more attuned to the needs of our customers," says managing director Andrew Goldfarb. "And, our clients will feel more comfortable with the support we offer them, because they share something with our staff. In essence, we serve our customers better because we can identify with them, and they feel more comfortable because they can identify with us."

Give More, Get More

Hanna Andersson Corp., a Portland, Ore., mail-order business, sells children's clothing. The 250-employee company also takes the clothes back when the children outgrow them. **Customers may return used items in good condition and get credit**—20% of the original price—toward their next purchase. The used clothes are donated to local charities, disaster relief organizations, and orphanages.

"Our Hannadowns program is a winner for everyone," says Diane Iosca, who handles public relations and publicity. "Children in need get good clothing. Parents teach their kids about sharing and helping others. And, our customers get a discount on future purchases. The Hannadowns program helps some customers justify the price of our products. They know it's a quality product that will last, and they get long-term savings."

The program has generated valuable publicity and developed loyal customers. Since 1984, more than 750,000 articles of clothing have been donated to charity. Customers feel good about being part of this effort.

"**A** delighted customer
is six times more likely
to repurchase your
product or service than
a satisfied customer."

JON ANTON
consultant with the
Center for Customer-Driven Quality, Purdue University,
and author of *Customer Relationship Management:
Making Hard Decisions with Soft Numbers*
(Prentice-Hall Inc., 1996)

Refer Customers to Your Competition

No small vendor can fill a customer's every need. But instead of playing dumb when clients must find another supplier, leading them to a competitor will improve your standing in the long run. That's what Frank Sennett of General Machine, located in Windham, Maine, has learned.

Sennett runs a shop that makes parts for electronics manufacturers. His customers sometimes need parts he either can't make or can't price competitively. So, he **helps them find another supplier**, even if it is a direct competitor. Although he might be turning away short-term business, he says it helps secure long-term advantages.

"Helping our customer gives us a 'team member' image," he explains. "If they're going to seek this information anyway, our position only gets better if we appear helpful, honest, and unthreatened by their request."

Acting like a partner encourages customers to communicate openly, too—that's the payoff. "We're better able to assess their needs and make early adjustments to our service to match changes in their operations," Sennett says. Two regular customers now include him in their new-product-planning sessions, as the plastic-parts expert. "I'm in on the ground level on new projects," he says, "so I can get the cream-of-the-crop jobs."

Cards for Compliance

If your customers must abide by certain regulations, try sending them the phone numbers of frequently called agencies. Chris White, marketing director for Environmental Compliance Testing (ECT), based in Rochester, Mass., tried this after getting repeated calls from his customers.

ECT tests the piping systems in hospitals that bring gases, such as oxygen and nitrous oxide, to patient and operating rooms. To ensure that a system complied with federal regulations, a hospital's director of engineering would routinely call White with compliance questions.

To ward off time-consuming calls, White **mailed Rolodex cards with the numbers of the relevant regulatory agencies**—and his company's name and number—to the directors of engineering at 2,682 hospitals nationwide. Now, when the hospitals suddenly have a problem or have to prepare to pass an upcoming inspection, "they panic, look up our name, see the agency's number, and call," White says.

ECT now mails about 3,000 pieces several times a year, hitting all of the hospitals in its 21-state market. "If your customers need to follow guidelines," he adds, "the cards will help them. They'll be grateful to you, and every time they look up a regulator's number, they'll see your name and be reminded of that."

Do Well by Doing Good

Warren Daniel, CEO and treasurer of The Bagelry, in Durham, N.H., believes in giving back to his community—that is, to his customers. With $2 million in sales and about 65 employees, the company tries to **give back 10% of its net profit each year**—a large figure, Daniel notes, for such a small company. In 1996, The Bagelry donated $10,000 to local groups and organizations.

The Bagelry and its four restaurants donate bagels to local sports teams, school lunch programs for low-income students, disadvantaged inner-city residents, homeless shelters, and other area organizations in the state's tiny seacoast. "It really improves employee morale and boosts customer loyalty" explains Daniel. "I believe companies should take a step in trying to help take up some of the slack, especially people in essential businesses like food and housing."

For those in other industries, Daniel suggests installing flowers or benches throughout the community or providing services to the elderly. "There are always needs in any municipal organization, and profitable companies always have the resources to help," he adds.

187
IDEA

Under Budget, Overjoyed

Everyone enjoys paying less than originally expected, and no one likes to pay more. Using this knowledge to your advantage can strengthen customer loyalty.

"We usually **estimate on the high side**, because I'd rather come in under budget than over budget," says Paul Benjamin, owner of the Benjamin Co., a public relations and advertising firm, in Hadley, Mass. "If you underbid on purpose just to get a job, you're going to have to justify an increase later," he adds. And that leaves a bad taste in the customer's mouth.

By estimating on the high side, Benjamin can come in below his estimate about 40% of the time, creating plenty of happy customers. "And when we charge less money than expected, they will often turn around and use the savings to hire us to perform some other work for them," he notes.

188
IDEA

Pampering Preferred

What customer doesn't enjoy **getting something for free**? If you go far for your customers, your customers will go far for you.

- Bob Morency, co-owner of R&D Ergonomics, located in Freeport, Maine, sells ergonomic products for office and industrial uses and consults with executives of companies on their ergonomic needs. When a prospective customer calls, Morency often arranges to make a personal visit free of charge.

  "I'll volunteer to go in and look at a couple of workstations, and I'll drop off some of our product for them to try," he says. More often than not, this leads to a sale. Morency also offers free, unlimited telephone support to customers, and he often receives faxes with a sketch of a workstation and a request for his advice on placement of ergonomic products.

- Norbert Johnston, owner of NBJ Management and Financial Services, in Brattleboro, Vt., says he travels 25 miles each way to his mechanic because of certain extra service he receives. "When inspection time is coming up or my car is due for an oil change, he calls me to remind me," says Johnston. "And my car also gets washed for free whenever it goes in for service."

189

IDEA

Bargain Basement

If you want to build customer loyalty, you have a key asset: You know your business better than your customers do. **Teach them how to save money when they do business with you**.

Norm Brodsky, CEO of CitiStorage, an archive-retrieval company, in Brooklyn, N.Y., does just that. When customers archive their records, they tend to lose track of them. The records often aren't of much use after several years have passed, and seldom do customers sort through old records to see what can be destroyed. Meanwhile, storage fees pile up as these customers continue amassing records.

CitiStorage saw a chance to help its customers by assigning a "destruction date" on every box a customer archives. When the date arrives, CitiStorage notifies the customer, who advises the company whether it should destroy the records. CitiStorage estimates that it has saved its customers as much as 40% of their storage costs.

Although Brodsky admits that sales are somewhat lower than they might otherwise be, this strategy reaps other rewards. Customers often stay with CitiStorage even when they might get a slightly cheaper rate somewhere else. Over the long run, that loyalty is worth much more to the business than the extra boxes.

"What is a customer?
A customer is the most important
person ever in this company
in person or by mail.
A customer is not someone to
argue with or match wits with.
Nobody ever won an argument
with a customer."

EXCERPT
from a wall poster
at L.L. Bean, in Freeport, Maine

IDEA

Daylight Saving

Multiplex, a manufacturer of automatic beverage-dispensing equipment, based in St. Louis, earns 40% of its $36 million in annual sales overseas. "We are always looking for ways to improve customer service," says J.W. Kisling, CEO. "There's E-mail, voice mail, and faxes for overseas customers, but one of the things they really appreciate is our **summer hours**."

During the summer months, Multiplex employees work an extra hour each day from Monday through Thursday, and on Friday they work a half day. "By Friday noon in St. Louis, it's 6 p.m. in the United Kingdom, 7 p.m. on the Continent, and Saturday morning in the Orient. We don't get many calls anyhow, so why not give customers longer hours of service when they can really use it?"

Company employees love the summertime perk, and customers can still count on a skeleton crew to answer the few calls that do come in. "Essentially, we've extended our workweek to 45 hours," says Kisling, who won the 1996 White House E-Star award for excellence in exporting.

Bagging Waste

For years, retailers have used bags or boxes to make it "convenient" for customers to carry their purchases home. To increasing numbers of environmentally-conscious consumers, however, more packaging means more waste—not more convenience.

In 1994, the retail division of Patagonia, a provider of high-tech outerwear, based in Ventura, Calif., adopted the goal of reducing point-of-sale packaging. This was in response to a growing customer perception that it's the right thing to do for the planet. At Patagonia's retail store, in Freeport, Maine, **customers who decline additional packaging at checkout become eligible to enter a monthly drawing** for four fleece pullovers. Forty percent of its customers decline the packaging.

As a result of the program, the Freeport store buys about 25,000 fewer bags each year. Customers like reducing the resources they use, and they get a chance to win valuable prizes.

Love It or Leave It

Throughout its 12-year history, California Pizza Kitchen, an 85-unit restaurant chain with locations in 20 states, has sought to push the boundaries of creative cuisine with innovations such as a BLT pizza and chicken-tequila pasta. Of course, it helps when customers are equally adventurous and willing to try new dishes.

"Our servers encourage customers not to be bashful," notes Julie Solomon, vice-president of training. To that effect, the Los Angeles-based company established a policy it calls the **Adventure Guarantee**. Printed at the bottom of each menu is a stamp with the message, "Be adventurous. Try something new. And if it doesn't thrill you, we'll replace it with your usual favorite."

"Servers have the authority to replace any meal," confirms Solomon, who adds that the number of meals returned has not increased at all since the guarantee began. "Bottom line: We want our customers to be thrilled with their dishes."

193

IDEA

Through a Fax, Sharply

Like many companies, Design Basics depends on the fax machine to immediately send customers the information they request. But, just because something is faxed doesn't mean it's okay for the presentation to be sloppy. The home-plan design firm, based in Omaha, is careful to ensure that the fine print and illustrations of its **plans are as legible on fax copies as on the originals**.

"We want our product literature to be easy on the eyes of our customers, because they spend a lot of time poring over plans and fine print," says Linda Reimer, Design Basics' president. To provide clients with high-quality material they can show a prospect, the creative department uses special line weights and typefaces; it also checks the quality of a faxed graphic before it goes into use.

The company also looks for little things to tack on for free that are easy to provide. Recently Design Basics started giving customers pocket-size miniplans so that they won't have to tote around the big, unwieldy blueprints all the time.

Reality Check

A poorly-written user manual or confusing orientation seminar can compound a customer's disappointment with a purchase. To ensure that your company's customer-communication tools are up to par, take a tip from a professional publisher of training materials and seminars. Sealund Associates, located in Clearwater, Fla., has **adapted the "beta test" routine**, popularized by software companies, to guarantee its customers completely debugged presentations and training manuals.

"If our manual is going to be used by bank-teller trainees, we hire a person from a temporary agency, with at least the education level and background a teller might have, to work through our material and see if it's easy to grasp," says Barbara Sealund, founder and president. The company depends on temp agencies for "substitute customers," too, and keeps a list of independent contractors whom they tap for the reality checks. Putting the company's materials through such a quality check costs Sealund approximately $300.

This is just one of several quality-control tests that Sealund Associates uses before handing over its materials to a customer. After debugging the material, an instructional designer makes sure that all the principles of adult learning are used and that the process runs smoothly. An officer of the company also reviews the total package to ensure that the customer gets top-quality materials on time.

195

IDEA

Check Here for Satisfaction

The old saying "retail is detail" even applies to customer service. Just ask Michael Horgan, a producer of corporate training videos, located in Harrisburg, Pa. Several years ago, Horgan launched a retail service, called Totally Video, which edits home videos from birthday celebrations, video Christmas cards, and other special-occasion tapes. Since Horgan can't be there personally to explain to novice video enthusiasts the various ways to jazz up and edit their material, he created a **multiple-choice worksheet to educate and guide customers**.

Says Horgan, "They aren't professionals, so they don't really know what to ask for to get the same quality of production you see on television." To steer customers toward producing a polished video they'll be happy with, the worksheet covers all aspects of professional video production, such as music, still photos, graphics, and incorporating old film footage. No matter who is working at the counter, the customer is certain to get good service. "We usually end up selling more services than the customer initially wanted," says Horgan.

Coast-to-Coast Hours

When a company's customers span time zones, aligning business hours with those of its customers can be difficult. But not for Milwaukee-based Tricom Funding. As founder John Leopold explains, "We want to mirror what it would be like to be an employee in his or her own office and to be able to respond to issues in as timely a fashion as possible—as if we were on-site."

Tricom functions as a service bureau for temp agencies, handling such back-office operations as accounts receivable and payroll processing. Even though its 140 customers are scattered across the country, the company's goal is to function seamlessly with its customers. To that end, Tricom **expanded its hours of operation** from 7 a.m. to 7 p.m., instead of the traditional 9 a.m. to 5 p.m. "Business doesn't stop for our West Coast clients at 3 p.m., and our East Coast clients couldn't get anything from us first thing in the morning," recalls Leopold. "Since they're our clients, they had a right to eight hours of access, so we responded to that." Leopold adds that most of Tricom's competitors don't respond to clients outside their own time zones. What's more, because Tricom staggers its staff, the expanded hours of operation do not cost Tricom any additional money. It's a zero-cost solution for Leopold, and a big benefit to his clients.

197
IDEA

Artists-in-Residence

For 40 years, Pro-Mark, a 28-employee firm, in Houston, has been manufacturing drumsticks for customers ranging from young novice drummers to professional musicians. For the past three years, the company has employed two **professional percussionists to staff its toll-free hotline**, rather than fill the position with traditional customer-service reps. "Our customers would much rather speak to an actual drummer," notes Kat Kelley, who works in both purchasing and customer service.

The drummers on the toll-free hotline go far beyond fielding questions about Pro-Mark products. "Kids just starting out in drum class love to get information over and above what they get from their teachers," notes Kelley. "And professional drummers appreciate discussing their problems with another percussionist—whether it's a finer point of technique or whether or not they're using the right stick in a given situation." When the percussionists are not helping out their fellow drummers, they are productive in additional ways: One is in charge of artist relations, and the other works in new-product development.

198
IDEA

Keeping the Dream Alive

When the sizzle of a sales pitch fizzles in the wake of the work necessary to fill the order, it's a great time to **offer customers a perk to keep them occupied and focused** on happier times ahead.

Dennis Brozak, founder and owner of Design Basics, a home-plan design firm, based in Omaha, provides his customers—the home builders—with a kit that allows future homeowners to dream about how they will decorate and furnish their new home.

In addition to serving Design Basics' customer's customer, the kit also serves the company's primary customer, the home builder. "They use the kit to help make a sale or find out if a plan needs modifications to accommodate a customer's grand piano," explains Brozak. "It helps home owners make their final decisions on wall color and finished goods in a timely fashion." Brozak has grown his company to $4 million in annual revenue, making it a market leader in its niche.

199 IDEA

Thank You for Holding

Customers placed on hold at the other end of a telephone line are a captive audience that many companies just can't resist. Consider how frequently company pitches and testimonials replace hold music or the nearly obsolete silence. Great American Business Products, a Houston-based supplier of forms to the automotive and real estate industries, decided its customers should be rewarded, rather than offended, if they were put on hold when calling its 800 number to order products.

Calls at Great American are usually answered within 20 seconds; during the wait, customers hear a recording informing them that they are entitled to a **bonus item for holding**. "It's not enough to have satisfied customers anymore," notes call-center trainer Sharon Robinson. "We want to amaze, astound, and astonish them, too."

Typically, bonuses may include a packet of extra forms, pens, or a coffee mug, but Robinson gives her sales representatives leeway to be creative. She recently sent a customer a gift certificate for dinner for two. The company spends approximately $10,000 per year on the gift items—an expense it feels is more than recouped by the goodwill customers and vendors spread by word-of-mouth. "Customers love it," notes Robinson, adding that 85% of them ask for their bonuses. The policy reduces the number of hang-ups, too. Many customers stay on the phone for no other reason than to find out what their bonuses are.

VII

"Everyone loses when service is poor. Customers lose. Employees lose. Senior managers lose. Suppliers lose. Shareholders lose. Communities lose. The country loses. Poor service has no redeeming virtue, nor does mediocre service, for that matter. Service excellence is more profitable, more fun, and more conducive to a better future."

LEONARD L. BERRY
professor of marketing, Texas A&M University, and author of
On Great Service: A Framework for Action
(The Free Press, 1995)

Cook Up Referrals

A new business in town can prosper on the strength of good referrals. For example, orthodontists commonly solicit referrals by taking dentists out to lunch or sending gifts to dentists' offices. Stephanie
Steckel, an orthodontist based in Dover, Del., decided against taking just
the dentist out to lunch, because 25% of referrals come from hygienists
and receptionists. The traditional approach of sending them office gifts
doesn't do much to demonstrate professional competence or improve the
timing of referrals. Her solution: **Lunch and Learn**.

Steckel brings lunch to the offices of dentists who are her best prospects
for long-term referrals. The lunch is simple—good deli sandwiches or
pizza—but the dessert is a diet-killing, home-baked specialty. After dessert,
Steckel provides a 30-minute continuing education seminar on advance-
ments in the field, the best age to refer different categories of patients, and
what conditions don't warrant a referral for orthodontia. She shows pictures and models of before-and-after work on mutual patients.

Exposure to Steckel's competence makes it easy for dentists and their
staff to make future referrals with confidence. Steckel has been told that
the dessert alone makes the occasion a winner. But there are other benefits. Steckel works with referring dentists to optimize the timing of referrals. Now, she receives fewer late, inappropriate, or early referrals, and the
number of appropriate referrals has increased. One dentist, who had been
referring one or two patients per month, referred 16 patients to Steckel the
first month after participating in Lunch and Learn.

Keep 'Em in Business

Should you abandon hope of repeat sales if your business customers have a high attrition rate? No way, says Larry Gaynor, CEO of a Farmington Hills, Mich., wholesale distributor of beauty products to salons. "Our customers rarely have a business background," says Gaynor. "They have to learn the hard way. We help them become business-oriented so they can stay in business."

Nailco Salon Marketplace was the first company in the industry to **establish a business ecosystem** providing services such as malpractice and liability insurance, 401K plans, credit-card financing, fax-on-demand material safety data sheets, and marketing support for signage and direct mail. The $32-million, 160-employee wholesaler offers customers these services at cost. "We leverage our suppliers to provide services that customers didn't know existed or didn't have access to," says Gaynor. "The ecosystem goes beyond exceeding customer needs—it anticipates them—which is the ultimate in customer service."

Program results have been spectacular. Fifteen thousand salons participate in at least one of the ecosystem services. "Customers write to us all the time saying that they love the services they receive," says Gaynor. "Retention of current customers has increased 30%, and order size has increased 35%. Referrals account for 85% of new customers, up from 70%." Gaynor notes that salon owners can choose among multiple suppliers with comparable selection and price. The long-term relationships forged by the ecosystem encourage them to choose Nailco.

It's Smarter to Barter

Madhu Sethi, founder and former owner of Innovation Computers, a computer dealer, in Deerfield Beach, Fla., took an innovative approach to handling a collection problem and gained unexpected benefits. One of the firms he dealt with each month owed him $80,000, but it was experiencing a cash crunch and couldn't afford to pay. So, the owner proposed giving him $150,000 worth of **credits through a barter service**. Sethi didn't even know what bartering was all about. "It was that or nothing," he explained. "Although I was disgruntled, I agreed to the deal."

Sethi admitted that agreement was one of the best business decisions he ever made. He held on to the business relationship, collected what might otherwise have been an uncollectible debt, and was able, meanwhile, to use that barter credit to advertise in several magazines that he normally would never have tried. Eventually, Sethi became an active member in a barter network, in part because there were several occasions when customers couldn't afford to pay their bills.

203

IDEA

A Bite of the Action

Delta Dental Plan of Massachusetts, an insurance company, based in Medford, Mass., convened a **"customer-partnership committee"** soon after the company had spun off from Blue Cross and Blue Shield in the 1980s. Committee members, some from big-name clients such as Polaroid and Gillette, were encouraged to talk candidly about their concerns. Later, the committee—which now meets quarterly and includes a rotating group of 20 customers—played a big role in crafting Delta's cash-back service guarantee, the company's best tool for bringing in and satisfying new customers. And with Delta's 1996 revenues at $231 million, the customer-partnership committee deserves its fair share of the credit.

204
IDEA

All the News That's Printed to Fit

Creativity for Kids didn't want its marketing newsletter pitched into a circular file. So, the Cleveland-based company cut its circulation in half by **weeding out all but retail customers, their reps, and hot prospects**. And newsletter staff members made an effort to feature stories they couldn't get elsewhere.

"The newsletter is enormously popular with our customers, who use it to help run their businesses," says Phyllis Brody, co-owner of the toy manufacturer and employer of 80 staffers. Three times a year, retailers in 4,000 business locations, as well as prospects, receive the newsletter. The publication routinely showcases innovative customer practices and passes on tips on how to boost sales. For example, one story explained how to orchestrate an in-store sales event in which retailers could run hands-on activities for parents and children. The story inspired about 600 stores to order up to 20 discounted promotional learning kits.

And, promotions such as the "Guru Contest," an annual challenge that asks readers to predict what the best-selling new Creativity for Kids products will be, encourage interaction with customers, draw attention to new products, and track readership.

Lending a Vending Hand

Share your commitment for great service with your vendors so that your customers receive great service, too. Champion Mortgage Co., in Parsippany, N.J., noticed a problem pattern when customers reported that their home equity loans or refinancing went well—except for the appraiser, attorney, or other outside vendor representing Champion. "The first person the customer meets is often the appraiser, and one of the last is the lawyer at closing," says Leigh Beumee, vice-president of marketing. "We need to rely on our vendors to provide great service so customers don't begin or end the process with a bad taste."

The mortgage company hired an outside services coordinator to **train vendors in customer service** and to find ways for Champion and its 45 vendors to work together better.

"Our vendors like having someone who sees their perspective and looks out for them, too. The coordinator is not positioned as the 'service quality police,'" emphasizes Beumee. "We've cross-trained employees for years but never included vendors. We now arrange for attorneys and closing representatives to sit in each other's shoes for half a day. It has opened eyes on both sides and has improved relationships. I know customer service has improved because customers now praise our vendors."

Champion created an "Outside Services Service Quality Award" to show its appreciation for the vendors' new commitment to customer service. The annual award goes to the firm or individual who receives the most praise from Champion customers. Winning vendors love the recognition, says Beumee, and it has become quite a competition among the various firms.

206

IDEA

Look In from the Outside

Stumped for ideas on how to improve your service? **Get a critique of your business from a third party.** Here are low-cost ways to get advice:

❧ *Find a local professional organization that sponsors business forums.* Haven's Candies, a candy manufacturer, in Portland, Maine, presented its business issues at a university-sponsored Enterprise Council meeting. "Receiving feedback from a panel of business experts and an audience of peers was an invigorating experience," says owner Bill Webster. "The discussion generated a number of practical ideas that I have put into practice."

❧ *Turn your business into a class project.* The Saint Lawrence Center Mall, a shopping complex, in Massena, N.Y., was concerned about its service to Canadian and American customers. The mall's management contacted a business-school professor and developed a case for students to research and analyze. Student teams provided the mall with term-project reports and recommendations.

❧ *Obtain free advice from business counselors.* Look in the telephone book for a nearby office of the Service Corps of Retired Executives (SCORE) or Small Business Development Center (SBDC).

Mutual Service

Are you sure your customers can use your products in conjunction with someone else's without frustration? Concern about product compatibility led to a partnership between Cell Marque Corporation, a biomedical reagent supplier, in Austin, and Ventana Medical Systems, a biomedical instrument and reagent manufacturer, in Tucson.

Ventana markets a well-respected laboratory instrument, but only sells a limited range of primary antibodies for use with the instrument. Cell Marque, which doesn't manufacture an instrument, supplies a wide range of primary antibodies. Unfortunately for the customer, it wasn't easy to use Cell Marque reagents with Ventana's instrument—time-consuming assembly and error-prone calibration were required. The solution was for Ventana to permit Cell Marque to supply its reagents in dispensers compatible with the Ventana instrument.

The two companies thus entered into a win-win partnership to **provide compatible products**, filling a void they both had in serving customers. The collaboration initially expanded the number of primary antibodies available to Ventana users by almost 70. As a result, Ventana's instrument is now more versatile, and Cell Marque's reagents are now easier to use. Customer response to the partnership has been overwhelmingly positive, says Paul Ardi, Cell Marque's product-sales manager, and the customer base for both companies has expanded significantly.

208 IDEA

Know Their Ingredients

To find ways to give customers what they want, you have to understand their needs. These needs are not always apparent, however. Chuck Davis, director of the Small Business Development Center (SBDC), in Portland, Maine, recommends **learning your customers' job descriptions** in order to adapt your services to their needs.

This practice paid off for Davis when he was CEO of a $20-million blueberry producer. The company's primary customers were professional buyers for large baking-mix companies. Given the unpredictable nature of the business, such as weather and world market demand, its customers had a difficult time performing duties such as budgeting and estimating delivery dates. "We investigated the job description of each of our primary customers," Davis says. "By knowing every aspect of their buyers' jobs, we were able to develop pricing arrangements and relay cost information to buyers in a manner that made their jobs easier. In short, we were able to satisfy our customers because we understood the demands of their jobs and how we could tailor our services to support them."

209

IDEA

Training by Degrees

The key to running a successful business is to hire the right people," advises Steve Burkhart, CEO and chairman of the board of Advanced MicroElectronics, in Vincennes, Ind. He also notes that "the learning curve of new employees is frequently long and results in slower service to customers." Advanced MicroElectronics, a computer maintenance company that earned $12.7 million in 1996, entered into a partnership with a local university to address these concerns.

The company went to Vincennes University, a local institution, and proposed developing a **two-year degree program that trained students to meet its needs**. Advanced MicroElectronics supplied state-of-the-art equipment to the school and assisted in putting together an up-to-date curriculum, while the university provided the teaching facilities and instructors. "When students graduate from the program, they're ready to start the job, and that results in better service to our customers," says Burkhart.

Fifty-nine of the company's 143 employees are graduates of the partnership program. Does the training lead to satisfied customers? "The majority of our 400 corporate customers are happy with our service," says Burkhart. "Revenues are projected to reach $24 million, double that of the previous year. The graduates from this program are some of the best in the field. Even large companies, like Intel, are eyeing them when they graduate."

"More than 80% of innovations
in high-performing companies
come from customers' ideas."

SHEILA KESSLER
president of Competitive Edge, in Fountain Valley, Calif.,
and author of *Measuring and Managing
Customer Satisfaction: Going for the Gold*
(Quality Press, 1996)

210
IDEA

Triumph with Trust

As director of manufacturing for Microtest, Michael Marinick serves customers by improving the quality, delivery, and cost of the company's network-productivity products. The $60-million, Phoenix-based company does this mainly by partnering with suppliers.

"If component suppliers share test data with us, and we share field failure data with them, we both improve our ability to identify and fix deficiencies in material, design, and processes," says Marinick. "Suppliers are naturally reluctant to share this information because it exposes their weaknesses. With one supplier, it took three years to build enough trust for both sides to be open with information. Now we share our product plans and sales information, and they share their internal costs and goals for growth. By **reviewing each other's businesses**, we are able to work together to reduce costs and improve forecasting and delivery. The symbiotic relationship really does allow both partners to achieve mutual objectives instead of pursuing mutually exclusive ones. The success of the relationship has moved us toward single-sourcing."

How does all this relate to customer service? "Customers want a product that works the first time and continues to work day after day," states Marinick. "By partnering with suppliers, we've cut field failure rates approximately in half and have reduced our cost to procure product. We can deliver a more reliable product to the consumer, at a lower cost."

You Guys Take the Cake

Customers don't make much of a distinction between our vendors and our company—if there is a problem with the service provided by a vendor, it reflects badly on us," says Cynthia Cattern, vice-president of training and development for Merit Property Management, based in Mission Viejo, Calif. This $10-million company, which provides property-management services for homeowner associations, also found that **expressing appreciation for vendors' efforts** goes a long way toward ensuring good customer service.

Cattern writes handwritten thank-you letters to vendors, and she nominates those that go above and beyond for the company's "killer cake" award: a decadent chocolate cake sent to one winner every month.

Current vendors are also invited to an annual appreciation night. Merit thanks vendors for their efforts and lets them know that their service to customers is instrumental in the company's success. "The response from vendors has been fantastic," says Cattern. "Vendors like meeting the people they've worked with only over the phone, and they feel like part of a team." She suggests planning an evening during which all vendors will feel comfortable. A fancy banquet didn't appeal to all of Merit's vendors, but a "Beers of the World" theme was a hit with everyone, from landscapers in T-shirts to lawyers in suits.

Company Loves Partnership, Gets Committed

Many small businesses distrust big business. So how was it that corporate-behemoth Motorola taught Bruce Bendoff's little company how to grow by trusting the giants it served?

Well, it didn't start that way. In the late 1980s, when Motorola announced that it planned to pare down its supplier base and turn the survivors into "partners," Bendoff feared that that was yet another ploy by a cost-conscious corporation to strong-arm its suppliers. Still, his sheet-metal-bending company, Craftsman Custom Metal Fabricators, in Schiller Park, Ill., had no choice but to start **sharing its secrets** with its huge customer: It depended on Motorola for roughly half its business.

Eventually, Bendoff started appreciating the benefits of the "unequal" marriage. With the two companies collaborating on parts design—from sketches on a napkin to shipment—cycle time dropped dramatically. "Something that took five weeks before," he said, "could now be produced in literally one or two days." And an adversarial, arms-length relationship slowly turned mutually supportive; Motorola even invited the Craftsman night-shift workers over to see how the company used its parts, and they obliged, roaring up on their motorcycles.

Bendoff was converted. In a fitful moment of bravery, he decided to make partnering a way of life, dragging his other customers and his own suppliers to the altar. The move was a good one: Craftsman has grown fivefold in the past decade, to $30 million in revenues.

213

IDEA

There's No Service Like Self-Service

Service after the sale, if thoughtfully planned, can be a boon to your business. Glenn Meltzer, president of Health-Tech Systems, in Hauppauge, N.Y., found ways to make customers more knowledgeable and generate excitement about his new products. He also increased referral business in the process.

Meltzer provides turnkey computer systems for dental offices. After he had sold a number of systems in Philadelphia, phone queries began to pour in. In response, Meltzer convened a group of customers to address common problems, and the participants decided to **form a user group**. The payoff was so great that Meltzer has since formed similar groups, in eastern Massachusetts, Long Island, Rhode Island, Washington, D.C., and Richmond, Virginia.

At each session, group members share ways to better utilize their systems. They also begin to call each other—rather than Health-Tech—when problems arise. Meetings soon take on the spirit of a self-help group.

The group costs Meltzer very little: some minor travel expenses, postage for a few letters, and a bit of time. And Meltzer has found that it generates another unforeseen benefit. "As a result of the user groups, we're selling many more upgrades," he says. Furthermore, Meltzer says, the company is getting new sales because of the groups. When group members socialize with their peers from other offices that are not yet computerized, they often talk positively about Health-Tech.

To Increase Referrals, Enrich Your Middleman

Many companies rely on other companies for customer referrals. For example, car dealers refer auto buyers to automobile insurers. Hotel clerks send their guests to restaurants. And real-estate agents match home buyers to mortgage companies.

Ernst Bartels, president of Executive Mortgage Bankers, in Farmingdale, N.Y., does not leave such referrals to chance. He has made his company the favored choice of real-estate brokers by helping them make money.

Mortgage companies routinely send agents fliers announcing new rates. But that's about all they do, and agents usually throw away the information. Looking for a better approach, Bartels **sent a hardcover binder to 50 agents in his area**. He told them that each week he'd send a one-page explanation of a certain type of mortgage, plus information on how Executive Mortgage could tailor that type of mortgage to different types of buyers. He encouraged agents to keep the sheets in the binder, noting that, over time, the collection would become a valuable reference.

In these weekly notices, Bartels's advice usually shows agents how buyers can afford more expensive houses. "I explain how a certain type of client can afford a $140,000 house instead of a $120,000 house," Bartels says. "I'm helping the agent find a way to make a higher commission."

Designed for Development

When publications specialist Jim Fawcette elected to launch a magazine to attract a readership of software programmers, he planned to tap that subscription base and the advertisers it drew for expansion into higher-margin areas, such as conferences. Among the first to sign on for ad space was, predictably, Microsoft Corp. After that, however, upfront cash support dwindled to nothing.

So Fawcette contacted potential advertisers and, rather than delivering a sales pitch, **solicited their participation in planning and designing the product** itself. To create a market and make his potential advertisers successful, he asked them what to do. These people represented "small companies working out of their basements, like myself, so they understood," said Fawcette. "They wouldn't be buying ads in a magazine, they'd be buying a market we'd developed together."

Fawcette acknowledges that their advertising support for a magazine that didn't even have a readership was critical in getting his company off the ground. Now, thanks to the way he served his advertisers, Fawcette Technical Publications, based in Palo Alto, Calif., estimates 1997 revenues at $24 million.

Reach Out and Teach Someone

Sheila West was expanding her archery business from retail to wholesale. But, archery dealerships were notoriously unreliable as retailers. They typically set up shop out of devotion to bow hunting, not commerce. And all too often those businesses failed.

For her company's sake, West decided to help her would-be customers become more reliable. She struck on the idea of a **trade show to instruct customers in business fundamentals**. Now, once a year, West's Archery Center International (ACI) stages the Pow Wow. A recent affair drew more than 100 manufacturers and 250 dealers. The total turnout topped 600 attendees.

"The seminars have made me a better businessman, no question about it," says Dick Adams, owner of Golden Arrow Archery, in Milan, Mich. Adams attended the first Pow Wow in 1987 and hasn't missed one since. "My sales have grown to $100,000, and a lot of that is due to the trade show. I've been to Pow Wow seminars on inventory control, cash flow, and how to compete with the catalog outfits." Adams is now such a devoted customer that he buys almost his entire product line from ACI. West's company has increased its annual sales from $540,000 to $3.8 million, while establishing a customer base of more than 800 dealers.

217
IDEA

Think Tanker

In the age of niche markets, it behooves niche-oriented providers to think outside the box of their own niche to really serve their customers. Yellowbird Trucking, a company that specializes in hauling international cargo, based in New Bedford, Mass., doesn't just try to provide quicker delivery times and lower prices than its competitors—it also involves other specialists who work with international freight, such as custom-house brokers and freight forwarders.

Assembling a brain trust can result in transforming the entire transportation logistics plan for a company, saving customers much more time and money than Yellowbird could provide on its own. In the process, customers become deeply bonded to Yellowbird for the long haul. For example, Ed Fitzsimmons, president of Yellowbird, teamed up with another specialist, a railhead company. By tinkering with a customer's current inland route and storing its container differently, the two companies saved the customer 50% on inland freight costs, shaved 10% to 15% off annual international transportation costs, and shortened delivery times. "If I hadn't linked up with this other specialist," says Fitzsimmons, "it would have been impossible to create such dramatic time and money savings for the customer."

VIII

"We are convinced
that advertising no longer sells
products today. People do. I think
a lot of people are wasting a lot of
money on advertising, and I don't
want to be one of them."

HORST RECHELBACHER
founder and CEO, Aveda Corporation, in Minneapolis
(*Marketing Masters: Secrets of America's Best Companies*
by Gene Walden and Edmund O. Lawler,
Harper Collins, 1993)

Dress Up Your Coupons

Coupons get customers in the door, but there are limits to their value. "Mass-mail coupons are costly, and they lose their effectiveness in attracting new customers once a local store is established," says Robyn Miller, general manager of eight Fantastic Sam's hair salons, in Louisville, Ky. She now uses **targeted coupon promotions**.

Stylists personally hand each customer a holiday discount coupon for the next visit. The celebration theme keeps the customer from inferring that services aren't worth full price. The holiday linkage also helps remind customers of the coupon's expiration date and encourages them to return in a timely fashion. A month without a holiday is turned into a "customer appreciation month."

Miller recruits new customers by mailing postcards to new homeowners, whose names are supplied free by the local paper. She also relies heavily on word-of-mouth communication. To get the word out, Fantastic Sam's teams up with local employers to offer discounts through company benefit programs. The employees learn about the discounts through their company's internal communications.

Do targeted promotions pay off? "You bet," says Miller. The $100 cost of printing coupons to distribute in the salons is nothing compared to the $6,000 it would cost for a single mass mailing. Since switching from mass-mail coupons two years ago, Fantastic Sam's has redeemed 5,000 additional coupons each year, and revenues are up $1 million.

Completely Accessible Facilities

Customer visits are a good marketing tool. "You never know when the next person in the door is a potential donor or a referring professional who just happens to be in the area," says Carl Mores, president and executive director of Cotting School, a Lexington, Mass., day school for children with developmental disabilities.

The school's literature features its open-door policy, and the school is prepared to show off its programs on any school day. The key is having a **plan in place to meet the needs of unexpected visitors**, to avoid disrupting students and teachers. Maintenance staff are trained to be welcoming and helpful to visitors they encounter on the grounds.

All employees understand the importance of creating a positive image and shift their priorities accordingly. To avoid potential problems, staff are expected to escort unknown visitors at all times. Receptionists have access to employee schedules, so they can direct visitors to the most appropriate available staff member.

The possibility of an unexpected visit from a parent or professional keeps the Cotting School's 110 staff members on their toes. And the open-door policy sends a strong message to the community that Cotting is confident of its service excellence.

IDEA

Generate Excitement

Want your customers to think you're special? Do something special for them. Bradley Co., a $2-million developer of software for managing business forms, has been holding annual user conferences since 1987. The three-day events are filled with seminars on software applications, discussions on customer-selected topics, and social events. Customers learn what Bradley can do for them, and Bradley has an exceptional opportunity to explore customer needs.

"It's the extra 5% that makes a conference extraordinary year after year," says John Zitzner, president of the Cleveland-based company. Following are examples of Zitzner's "extra 5%":

Keep 'em guessing. The location of the banquet is kept a mystery.

Add the unexpected. One year, the president and staff personally greeted guests at the airport and carried luggage to a waiting van.

Recognize customers. Two or three individuals and one firm are honored with customer appreciation awards. Bradley employees vote on which customers went above and beyond by training their staff on Bradley systems, or by giving extensive references to prospective clients.

Invite the right people. Most attendees are the regular folks punching away on Bradley computer systems. The business trip may be the only one many will take all year—and likely the only one during which they'll stay at a fancy hotel. The trip should feel like a big deal to them.

"Little things have an impact," says Zitzner. "When I travel to client locations, I invariably see our customer award on the wall and the group photos taken at the banquet pinned to cubicle walls. People keep the things that have meaning for them."

Good Psychology

Everyone knows the auto-repair business has an image problem. "Customer satisfaction is hard to achieve when the industry's revenues are based on large, unexpected, and unwanted expenses," notes Peter Fink, president of Certified Transmission, headquartered in Omaha. Undaunted, Fink built his company around the concept of turning grudging, skeptical prospects into repeat customers who refer friends.

Fink pays as much attention to the customer's state of mind as to the state of the car's transmission. Here's what he does to **create a culture of integrity that relieves customer anxiety**:

1. Contribute to scholarships and local nonprofit organizations.

2. Use reassuring language in company literature—for example, the "Certified" company name; frequent use of words such as "reliability," "quality," and "expert."

3. Be a good neighbor. Invite business neighbors to your open houses and make sure your building's exterior and grounds are well maintained.

4. Display employee training certificates and company awards where they'll be easy to read.

5. Eliminate commissions on sales and other incentives to sell customers more than they need.

6. Solve problems quickly and fairly. Overdeliver on guarantees.

7. Give customers access to top management. Provide customers with the president's or owner's cellular-phone number before complaints turn into serious problems.

Giveaways for Good Customers

How do you reward customers for buying more? Discounts and favorable terms on high-volume purchases are a start. Another way to encourage customers to spend more is to **give them a gift from your excess inventory** when their purchase amounts reach a specified figure.

Barb Todd, owner of a $21-million mail-order business, in Portland, Ore., knows it works. Each time a customer spends $250 or more on a single order from her Good Catalog, she sends a gift. Although it's called the Really Outrageous Gift Program, the system is hardly excessive, because she selects gifts from leftover inventory or product samples and ships them with a personalized letter. The average gift has a $75 retail value, yet it is really worth about $15 at the warehouse sale where it would otherwise be sold. Todd is glad to give up a little something to encourage large sales. "It costs me more money to process ten $25 orders," she says.

According to Todd, the freebie's effect is dramatic. Within a few months of starting the program, the gift recipients' response rates to mailings rose from 5% to 25%, while the amount of their average purchases increased from $100 to $300.

Helping Kids Is the Ticket

Sometimes the best way to satisfy customers is to help them do something nice for someone else. The Orlando Magic professional basketball team **gives season ticket holders the opportunity to donate unused tickets to disadvantaged youth**. "Customers feel great about themselves and about our company, knowing that their unused tickets are providing opportunity for ill and underprivileged youth in the Orlando area," says Jamey Lutz, quality and customer-service specialist for the Orlando Magic management company.

The company—which also owns a minor-league hockey team, team sportswear retail stores, and a large sportsplex—works with three local organizations serving disadvantaged youth to distribute the tickets.

More than 250 tickets are donated each year. "These giveaways have made a lot of kids, employees, and customers happy" says Lutz. "The satisfaction customers derive from sending these kids to a game rivals that of experiencing the 'Magic' themselves."

224

IDEA

To Know and to Serve

Pro-Mark, a $10-million drumstick maker, based in Houston, **advertises in trade publications** such as *Modern Drummer* to get to know its customers. The ads help bring the 40-year-old family business closer to its retail customers, test-market new products, and build brand loyalty. Pro-Mark won five awards in *Modern Drummer's* 1995 consumer poll. Here are a couple of Pro-Mark's campaigns.

- *Finding test-marketers.* One ad, offering free product samples in return for customer feedback, generated more than 3,000 responses. The new test-marketers have proved to be conscientious reviewers. For the first two years of the project, the company boasted a 100% response rate.

- *Promoting new products.* When Pro-Mark wanted to draw attention to former Pearl Jam drummer Dave Abbruzzese's new autographed drumsticks, it printed a coupon allowing readers to buy them for $5 and enter a contest to win a chance to hang out with Abbruzzese. More than 3,500 people responded, and Pro-Mark added the names to its catalog mailing list.

Clients Are Made, Not Born

Hanson Galleries, a United States art dealer with galleries in four cities, works hard at developing its clientele. In keeping with the Hanson Galleries method, a seller needs to **dissipate the customer's fears**. This includes:

- *Education.* As a rule, the more that potential customers know about whatever you're selling, the more of it they're likely to buy. Clients have to be educated, and that's part of the seller's job.

- *Protection.* Any art purchase, especially big-ticket items, represents buyer risk: he or she may be paying for something that's not worth the price. A smart seller not only eliminates the risk but also reduces the buyer's perception of risk. Guaranteed buy-backs give buyers the security they need to follow through with the purchase.

- *Expectation.* People tend to accept established norms—buying patterns, for instance—in which consumers purchase works of art one at a time. If one piece of art is all they expect to buy when they visit the showroom, you'll have to work on changing their expectations before they'll buy two.

- *Satisfaction.* You've educated your customers, hedged their risk, and changed their expectations. Now you have to follow through with product or service packages that appeal to and satisfy the needs of your customers.

226
IDEA

Feathers in Her Cap

Ann Withey, owner of Annie's Homegrown, a $3.5-million Sausalito-and-Boston-based macaroni-and-cheese manufacturer, boasts a database of 75,000 customer names. How does a company that never sees the customers face-to-face achieve this? Here are a few ways that Withey **connects with her customers**.

- *Coupons.* Annie's encourages word-of-mouth marketing by sending discount coupons to customers' friends. Withey writes back to 25 customers a week and sends form letters in response to approximately 1,500 customers each month. Customer information from the letters she receives is entered into the database.

- *Annie's home number.* "We want people to realize there's a real Annie," says Deborah Churchill Luster, president of the company. Withey gets about 50 calls per day from customers. She asks callers for feedback about the product and about in-store promotions.

- *The Internet.* Annie's Web site lures almost 400 visitors and collects approximately 30 E-mail messages every week. The Web site address (URL) is printed on the package.

- *Packaging.* "Until recently, the only advertising we did was on the box," says Luster. Last spring the company started running radio and bus ads, and it now publishes a company magazine.

- *Gift offers.* Free bumper stickers spread the company's environmentally conscious message, get people to pick up the product, and encourage customers to write in.

Be everywhere, do everything, and never fail to astonish the customer.

MOTTO
Macy's, a retailer owned
by Federated Department Stores Inc.

Show and Tell

Mike Smith, owner of California Pools of Arizona, says he has taken his Mesa, Ariz., pool-building business from "zero to the second largest pool company in the world over the past nine years." How? According to Smith, his company is obsessed with satisfying the customer.

Smith impresses customers with a down-to-earth, **15-minute videotape created for them and guaranteeing their satisfaction**. "A lot of companies waste money on glitzy, poorly acted videos that no one wants to watch," says Smith. "Ours is a nuts-and-bolts home movie with the owner telling how it is. We didn't fix up stumbles in speech or stage anything that wasn't genuine."

Smith doesn't disguise the construction project's disruption to customers' lives, because he wants his customers to have realistic expectations. Smith also showcases finished projects in the video to show customers the range of pool features available to them. "I don't want anyone to say at the end that they wished they had known about some feature they could have included in their design," Smith says. "It's surprising how a short video makes sure that people don't miss any features. It opens their minds to the possibilities of what can be done."

The video helps new customers develop a rapport with Smith—they already trust him and treat him like someone they know.

228 IDEA

Share Your Intellectual Capital

You're an expert on your industry. So, why not package that expertise for customers? Flexible Personnel, a $56-million staffing company, located in Fort Wayne, Ind., transformed its employment-law know-how into a labor-law seminar. "We thought this would be worth a lot more to our customers than the coffee mugs and key chains our industry typically hands out," says president Doug Curtis.

Clients agree. Nearly 800 customers and prospects came to the most recent seminar (one free all-day session) armed with questions about complex labor laws, such as the Americans with Disabilities Act. A paid consultant and Flexible's lawyer led the discussion.

After seminars, attendees often call Flexible with more questions. Each of its 38 field offices averages one call a month. Customers can contact Flexible's lawyer with more complex queries. The company also covers labor-related topics in its quarterly newsletter, which is mailed to 15,000 customers and prospects.

Serving as a resource to customers does take time, but it's a great prospecting tool. After the last seminar, the agency received 45 new job orders—totaling roughly $500,000—and earned the business of a customer that Flexible had pursued for three years.

A Piece of the Puzzle

Elms Puzzles, in Harrison, Maine, makes a product that's too expensive for most people—a 500-piece handcut wooden jigsaw puzzle that might cost $800. So, in 1991, the $250,000 company came up with a plan to provide the ultimate customer service: **access to the product for people who can't afford to buy it**.

Customers can join the Puzzlers Club for a $50 one-time fee and rent puzzles by the week. Rental fees range from $20 to $110, depending on the number of pieces. Membership has grown from 25 members, generated from an initial mailing using the company's database, to 200 members in 1997. As an added service, club members are the only people eligible to buy used puzzles at a steeply discounted rate.

Elms vice-president Fred Stuart notes that the rental club makes wooden puzzles available to people who love them but can't afford to keep them. "It's also been good for us. Sales have increased dramatically. Rentals are a profitable end of the business, and they help regular sales because rentals get our puzzles into homes where friends and neighbors see them."

Expanding Horizons

It's no secret that educating prospective customers on how to make the most of a product increases both sales and satisfaction after the sale. Mickey Robertaccio, owner of Sandy Hollow Herb Company, in Wilmington, Del., recommends the following techniques to increase customer knowledge:

Offer classes for a nominal fee. Select topics from customer requests. "Customers are amazed by the number of uses for a single herb," asserts Robertaccio. "The classes really help them get the most out of their purchases." They also function as a form of market research. By paying attention to customer interests and questions, staff learn how to provide better service.

Create ministores within the store. Each of these ministores can be staffed with a specialist. While staff can answer basic questions about all areas of the store, customers are more likely to engage in conversation with people who project expertise in a specific area, such as folk healing or aromatherapy.

Send newsletters to customers. Most companies are adamant about maintaining a consistent look and feel to each issue of a newsletter. Robertaccio takes a different approach. Three times a year, different staff members write the newsletter. The process of producing a newsletter is developmental for employees. Customers feel connected to employees, because each issue conveys the unique knowledge and personality of the writer. These ties are reinforced when customers with questions seek out the writer on their next visit to the store.

231
IDEA

Friend, Not Foe

Glen White, owner of Scientific Information Services, in Fort Worth, knows exactly what his newsletter should accomplish: six new contracts a month. White's business—a management-consulting firm that advises clients on hazardous-waste regulations—is not the stuff of glamorous ads. It's so specialized, it borders on the obscure: "Not many people would know where to begin to look for a hazardous-chemical management consultant."

Advertising and cold calling produced meager results. His prime customers, chemical-company managers, viewed his company as an arm of the government, an enemy instead of an ally, until White began publishing a monthly **newsletter chock-full of information about new laws and industry trends**. It built trust, warmed sales prospects, and soon began yielding the sought-after six new accounts a month.

A newsletter doesn't have to be expensive. Many word processing programs have features that can help you produce professional-looking newsletters. Here are a few more money-saving tips:
- Keep it to one or two pages
- Use your everyday stationery
- Photocopy it
- Use your own mailing list
- Send it using bulk-rate postage

Pest-Free—Naturally

All-natural biogardening: Can it exist? We're talking organically correct fertilizer here, not to mention toxin-free insecticides and herbicides that harness insect-fighting agents existing in nature. Ringer, a manufacturer, in Bloomington, Minn., produces these products and is spreading the word. Ringer educates its customers about the advantages of biogardening with an **array of free brochures that contain nary a product—or price**.

"We've always been an education-intensive business, because what we're selling is different," said Rob Ringer, son of company founder Judd. "People don't know the whole natural approach." Ringer, which registers annual sales of $14 million, enlightens its customers as a presales service, which eventually boosts revenues.

What do customers conclude from this approach? That Ringer's campaign for ecological sensitivity is genuine and trustworthy, not artificial and profit-driven—and that the company is more interested in the quality of its products than in the manipulation of its image. The direct manner with which its claims are offered contributes to the company's credibility.

233
IDEA

Fishing for Big Ones

Owners of small companies usually figure that if they can prove themselves with a few smaller clients, they'll be able to attract bigger accounts. Not Jeremy Barbera. He started at the top, then worked his way down.

Barbera, founder and CEO of Marketing Services Group, located in Manhattan, helps clients design databases and implement direct-mail campaigns to attract new customers. When he started his firm in 1987, he decided to go after high-visibility "class acts" such as orchestras and museums. After Barbera set up an appointment to see a new prospect, he researched the company extensively to discover its specific marketing problem, then **devised a solution to present at the first meeting**. With his prospects prepared to explain their problem, Barbera impressed them by beating them to the punch.

Once Marketing Services Group had signed a big name, wooing others in the same field became easier. When Barbera won the account for Carnegie Hall, in New York, other major auditoriums signed on, such as the Wang Center for the Performing Arts, in Boston. After he snagged *Crain's Chicago Business,* several smaller business magazines followed. "If you can get number one," he says, "numbers two through 10 are a lot easier."

234
IDEA

Power of an Open Book

Here's a new argument for opening your company's books: It can be a hot customer-service tool. Unipower Corp., a Coral Springs, Fla., electronics manufacturer, has discovered just how advantageous it can be for a private corporation to **publish its annual report**.

The company's annual report details sales, number of employees, net income, and balance-sheet information. But the real meat, says marketing chief Ed Schneider, is a four-page section called "Understanding Unipower" that lists the company's markets, sales channels, competitors, and top 25 customers.

Why go to such lengths? "It tells our customers they're doing business with a real company," explains Schneider. "They can look at the sales history and say, 'My God, they're growing, and they have inventory under control.'" He adds, "We want to impress customers and intimidate our competition. Everyone is teaming up with a limited set of suppliers. You have to set yourself apart."

Careful to act as a public company would, Unipower's founders offer one caveat to the open-book strategy: be prepared to back up your claims. Since publishing its first report in 1991, the company has grown 933% over a five-year period.

235
IDEA

Smile for the Camera

Most people like to have their picture taken. It makes them feel important. So, **turn photo opportunities into quality promotion pieces** for your business.

At Eriez Magnetics, a manufacturer of magnetic laboratory and metal-detection equipment, the receptionist lined up visiting customers underneath a sign of the company logo and snapped their picture. "It's just our way of saying thank you," said Chet Giermak, president and CEO. "We're complimented that you would come all the way to Erie, Pa., just to see us."

The photos also served a practical purpose. Giermak sent one to visitors with a cover letter reminding them of the reason for the visit and the people with whom they met. He slipped the photo into a cardboard frame with the company's mission statement on the back. It only took a minute to dictate the letter, and each complete package, including the stamp, cost only $2. On receipt, several potential customers made a second sales appointment.

Interns as Interpreters

In an ethnically diverse area, business owners often have a difficult time connecting with potential clients because of language, cultural, or religious differences. Eric Cohen Associates, located in New York City, which designs insurance and employee-benefit plans for businesses, had found it hard to reach the hundreds of local Chinese, Indian, Israeli, Pakistani, Russian, and other ethnic businesses. Then it dawned on Eric Cohen and his two employees that **hiring college students of these nationalities as interns** might help. He now regularly scouts New York, Columbia, and Yeshiva universities, taking on two interns each semester.

The intern's role is to build rapport, explain things to clients in their native language, and identify the personal concerns of the prospective clients. "Business owners in ethnic areas often distrust people who are not from within that community." Cohen explains. "But when they see the intern with me, that changes." Once Cohen develops a business relationship, cultural differences become less of an issue—although sometimes Cohen calls the intern back months later to participate in an important meeting, paying for his time. "In the last two to three years, the interns have doubled my business," he says.

IDEA

Sponsorship Supports Success

Nine years ago, Bennett Gibbs of Bennett's Cycle, located in Minneapolis, sent a couple of mechanics from his retail store to lend a hand at a bicycle race sponsored by the American Lung Association. Gibbs figured that in addition to helping a good cause, his mechanics could hear what bike enthusiasts had to say about his shop—and his competitors. So Gibbs began to get involved in various community events. Today he participates in 30 annually. But Gibbs has learned firsthand that charitable time and money can amount to a big loss unless you **make your sponsorship visible** before, during, and after an event.

For example, at a recent Iron Man ride, a 100-mile event for 5,700 hard-core bike riders, Bennett's opened its doors for registration prior to the event, offering participants six seminars on fitness and bicycle maintenance. At the ride, the company gave away bags filled with bike accessories and discount coupons on bike tune-ups and helmets. Also, printed on the bags was an offer for a 20% discount on all the merchandise shoppers could fit into their bags. Within a week, 30 participants had come into the store. Shortly after last year's Iron Man ride, Gibbs discovered that 2,500 participants bought goods at Bennett's Cycle. "I support them, and they support us," says Gibbs, whose business has grown into a 22,000-sq.-ft. retail and repair operation with annual revenues of $3.5 million.

Creative Incentives Capture Clients

Aunique incentive can close a sale, gain someone's trust, or motivate a customer to change. In selecting gifts for your clients, choose something that is out of their reach. For example, identify seasonal or regional incentives, such as a box of white Bing cherries or a case of California Merlot shipped directly from the winery. Listen carefully to what your client appreciates during ongoing conversations—the impact of a **unique and personal incentive** is that much greater.

Case in point: Jack Jacchino, managing partner of the J.P. Burns Group—a strategic development consulting company, in Islip, N.Y.—was having trouble convincing managers at a paper mill in a remote Maine town to implement his ideas. They decided to discuss their concerns over dinner at a local Chinese restaurant, which the managers said had great food. "It was the worst," recalls Jacchino, who was spoiled on authentic Chinese cuisine from New York City's Chinatown. He told them, "If you try the steps I'm recommending, I'll ship you $200 worth of the best Chinese food in the country." They successfully implemented his suggestions, Jacchino sent the reward, and the managers were delighted.

239
IDEA

Tell Them a Story

Eva Lynne, who runs the World Market, in Northampton, Mass., has found that customers like a colorful tale. The World Market sells imported craft items, everything from tabors to shadow puppets. Each time a new piece comes in, Lynne types up its history, puts it in a loose-leaf book, and expects her salespeople to learn it.

Storytelling turns what would otherwise be an awkward encounter into a conversation. "The customers like it because they're learning something," says Lynne. "They ask questions, which allows us to **convey information without sounding like a sales pitch**. We get all the senses involved. As customers hear a story, we show them details on the piece. We let them hold it and smell it. They feel good, they buy, and they also look forward to coming back for another story. I've even given tours of the entire store because customers were too intrigued to leave."

"Great service takes hard work, perseverance, and a good client— a client who shares information and treats our relationship as a partnership, not as a vendor relationship."

BOB BERMAN
director of communication for Market Facts Inc.,
in Arlington Heights, Ill.

A Freebie Worth Copying

f you have a new business or want to increase sales in your store, copy an idea from J.C. Halbrooks, manager of Office Plus, a print shop, in Foster, R.I.: Invite people to make **copies on your duplicating machine for free**. You will probably get more back in new business than you give away.

Halbrooks lets people make up to five copies a day at no charge. "Everybody needs copies," he says. "It generates traffic and goodwill—and gets us out of making small change."

The little step has had even bigger results for Halbrooks: It's low-cost advertising for the store. "People talk about it—it's free," he says. "It spreads our name around the neighborhood." What's more, he notes, the drugstore down the street charges five cents a copy, so people stop just to get five freebies.

The something-for-nothing strategy gives customers a chance to see that the reproduction quality is excellent at Office Plus, and when they have more demanding jobs, they return. Halbrooks doesn't worry about whether customers are sneaking a few extra copies; the ploy has increased walk-in business and helps people remember the Office Plus name. "Besides," he says, "some people feel guilty. They end up leaving money anyway."

Fake It Till You Make It

Being new and tiny, how do bootstrappers **assure suppliers and customers of their ability to pay or deliver**? By convincing them they're not new and tiny. "One thing I realized very quickly is that people want to see fancy offices, fancy letterhead, fancy everything," says Michael Kempner, founder of MWW/Strategic Communications, in River Edge, N.J.

He didn't have fancy anything, but he had a friend in advertising who did. Kempner moved into the friend's office at no expense, understanding that his public-relations firm would steer advertising in the friend's direction. He even moved in on the ad company's name: "I put a slash on it, added 'Strategic Communications,' and looked like I was part of a big company. It was all a mirage at the beginning. As far as my clients knew, here I was with a fancy name in a fancy office. Those were important, or people wouldn't hire me. This way, they came upstairs and saw 40 employees and thought they were working for me. I never told clients those people didn't work for me, and they never asked."

Since then, the company's adjunct, MWW, has gone under. Kempner's major problem: "Now that the company's not fake anymore, I'd like to change the name; I hate it, but it's too late."

Building Blocks to Great Relationships

It's not every day you sit in the office of a business executive whose desk features a crystal paperweight shaped like a baby's alphabet block. "Sure, it's a little unusual," said Sandra Burud, president of Burud & Associates, in El Segundo, Calif., one of the nation's leading child-care benefit consulting firms. "But that's what makes it such a great gift for our clients."

In past years, Burud has presented a Waterford crystal baby block to fewer than five corporate or institutional clients, as a gift in honor of the "ongoing, truly exemplary" relationships they've built with her firm.

The baby block was a perfect gift. "You know immediately that it's about children, which is our one and only focus in this business," says Burud. "And because it's Waterford, there was a strong message of quality—that is the goal in everything we do. Best of all, because it's something that's out of place in an office, the **gift becomes a conversation piece**." With the baby block now out of production, clients receive a gold pin, depicting a child's hand with an adult's hand, symbolizing the work performed on behalf of parents and children.

In past years, her entire contact list received a calendar produced by the Children's Defense Fund, a Washington, D.C., advocacy group. Every now and then "just for fun or to say thanks for something," she sends out baby bottles filled with pink and blue candies.

Uncompromising Standards

In the early 1990s, Ohio insurers began aligning themselves with a handful of auto body repair shops in each market. Shops that didn't like the insurers' rules faced a choice: either make concessions in quality, or find a new way to bring in business.

In January 1993—against the recommendations of many associates—Bob Juniper Jr., owner of Three-C Body Shop, in Columbus, bought airtime at a local radio station. "This is Bob Juniper," he began. "There's a growing problem in the collision-repair industry that seriously affects every vehicle owner in central Ohio. Quality collision-repair standards are being systematically destroyed by insurance direct-repair programs. These programs, which encourage the use of imitation parts, cheap labor, and other concessions, were designed by insurance companies for their own benefit, to keep their costs down, not yours. We have never participated in any of these programs, and we never will. Why? Because when it comes to repairing your car, we will **never compromise the safety and quality of your repairs**."

Among insurance agents and competing body shops, the reaction was predictably negative. However, the ads had resonance among customers. Three-C's name recognition and business soared as a result of its concern for customer satisfaction. In June 1993, the company was in operation around the clock; by year-end, sales had more than doubled, to $2.7 million. In 1995, Three C's sales more than doubled again, to $5.5 million, and climbed higher to $6.2 million a year later. Juniper notes that 75% of customers said they first heard about the company on the radio.

244

IDEA

Giving Where It Counts

Do your customers really need another box of chocolates or corporate knickknack during the holidays? For years, General Engineering Laboratories, a consulting firm, located in Charleston, S.C., showered its customers with wine, cookie bouquets, and candy at holiday time. But in 1994, General Engineering decided a change was in order: It altered its holiday giving practices to be more consistent with the philosophy of corporate giving that it practiced throughout the rest of the year.

"Our company is very active in the community, and we give significant donations to many organizations, from health and human services to educational and environmental," explains David McNair, vice-president for corporate development. Now, instead of sending the traditional year-end gift, the company makes a **special contribution to charities in honor of its clients**. A card is enclosed that says, "In thanksgiving for our many blessings, and in honor of our clients, we are making a special holiday contribution to the _____ organization. Wishing you a blessed Christmas Season!" Each year, General Engineering donates "an amount in the thousands" that varies each year, depending on the year's profits and the number of charities to which the company is contributing.

"While it's difficult to quantify the direct benefits of such a program," observes McNair, "many customers comment that our gift is thoughtful and refreshing—and it says a great deal about the type of company we are."

Free, Slim, and Specific

Sending less product literature to customers can actually be a more efficient way to communicate with them and service their needs. Like other companies in its niche, Design Basics, a home-plan design service, based in Omaha, used to sell catalogs to builders showing home plans of every style and size, in prices from $3.95 to $100 per catalog. Now, instead of overwhelming customers with needless information and charging them for it, Linda Reimer, president of the design firm, saves them the hassle by **custom-binding sketches and layouts of specific interest to each customer** and sending them on a complimentary basis.

Reimer figures the savings in printing and postage alone will offset the incidental revenue stream generated through sales of home-plan catalogs. Already, Design Basics sells more than $4 million worth of actual home-plan blueprints per year.

Payback Time

When the end of the month arrives, sometimes the only type of service a customer receives is an invoice. But Fred Barnes, founder of Working Assets Long Distance Service, in San Francisco, looked at his company's billing statement as a way to elicit strong customer bonds in the fiercely-competitive telecommunications industry.

Working Assets gives customers an **easy, painless, and regular way to donate to a variety of causes** and charities. On each month's statement, customers can choose to round up the amount of the payment due and have every penny of the excess funds donated to the charity of the month. At the end of the year, customers receive statements detailing the total amount of their charitable contributions for the year, for their tax records.

"We choose causes that we believe will be popular with our customers, on the basis of their past record of giving," says Laura Scher, president of Working Assets. Scher reports that the company has grown to $100 million in revenues and has collected $3 million in donations for nonprofit organizations in 1997 alone.

IX

"Great service companies,
regardless of the nature
of their business, couple
the basics of service
with the art of surprise."

LEONARD L. BERRY
professor of marketing, Texas A&M University,
and author of *On Great Service: A Framework for Action*
(The Free Press, 1995)

Customer Comfort

Running the Sun City, Ariz., Audiology and Hearing Aid Center has sensitized owner Diane Shultz to the fact that a number of elderly clients of this $500,000 business have limited mobility and experience considerable physical discomfort. Her **concern for the physical comfort** of her patients has resulted in positive changes that are appreciated by young and old alike.

- New waiting-room chairs with sturdy arms and high seats make sitting down and getting up easier for frail or heavy clients, who don't want to struggle up out of cushy sofas.

- Since metal door handles can be hot in summer and cold in winter, hand-knitted handle covers—a customer suggestion—solved the problem and added a touch of homeyness.

- A choice of sugar-free candy, which 10% of Shultz's patients enjoy, is offered in the reception area.

- Like fast-food and banking customers, clients appreciate a drive-up window to drop off repairs or pick up batteries. The window is low enough so that patients don't have to stretch awkwardly, and the service provider doesn't tower over the customer.

- A mint, handed out with the receipt, keeps the encounter friendly. And, says Shultz, these touches keep customers coming back.

A Visit in Time Saves Nine

Small mishaps can sour the tone of otherwise successful visits from clients and prospects. Craig DeLuca, president of Executive Perspectives, located in Brookline, Mass., knows the value of a smoothly run client visit. "A customer likes to be treated like a king or queen. It's human nature," says DeLuca. That's why his management training firm has designated a **client concierge who coordinates the minutiae of a visit** using a detailed checklist. Specific client requirements are thoughtfully attended to before they become problems, and the client has a personal visit coordinator to contact if needed.

The client concierge also acts as timekeeper, ensuring that a meeting or presentation moves along according to schedule. Current and prospective clients alike appreciate that they will make other appointments on time. A clear title for such a role helps all employees in the firm treat the function of visit coordination as seriously as they should.

How to Win with Pins

When special clients visit Harte-Hanks Kansas City, in Lenexa, Kans., all 300 employees wear **customized welcome buttons** with the client's name or logo. Buttons such as "Proud to Be in the Breeders Club" for a Ralston-Purina visit are made in the graphics department for less than $1 each. Paper signs slipped into reusable name tags cost even less. The customized buttons make the client feel at home, says Henry Lammers, vice-president of marketing for this $30-million database marketing company. More effective than memos, the buttons also heighten employee awareness of the visit's importance so that the company will put its best foot forward.

It's Personal

Everyone likes something extra—it's human nature," says Mary Reynolds, owner of Around Austin, a $300,000 company specializing in tours of the Texas state capital and special events in the area. The first hotel to put a mint on the pillow did something special, but this has become the norm. People now expect freebies, so a little something extra is special only if it's personalized.

Reynolds says that creativity is required to **provide her customers an unexpected pleasure**. It doesn't cost much to make people feel good about themselves, she says, just some personalized attention. A few examples include:

- An unscheduled scenic stop for a group showing interest in the local landscape.
- Substituting chocolate cake for the preplanned apple pie when serving a group of self-proclaimed "chocoholics."
- Presenting a Texas bandana to a group coordinator who had to be coaxed to sit on a longhorn steer—but felt great about it afterward.

What's the payoff of personalized surprises? People are more likely to remember a trip as special if they get more than they thought they were paying for. Memories create repeat business and referrals. And, of course, valuable repeat business makes it easier to get to know the customer and provide personalized service.

When No Tip Is a Good Tip

Many hotel guests dislike fumbling for change and figuring out how much and how often to tip whom. Room service, concierge, bellhop, doorman, and cleaning staff: All that tipping at better hotels adds up to an unnecessary nuisance. But at San Francisco's Inn at Union Square, employees haven't accepted tips since June 1995, when a customer's suggestion for a **no-tipping policy** was adopted.

General manager Brooks Bayly's logic was that the nuisance of tipping was inconsistent with the hotel's mission statement designating excellent service as the highest goal. Customers love not having to worry about tipping, says Bayly, and they no longer have to get change for tips at the front desk, which used to happen five to 10 times a day.

Wages were increased to compensate for average annual tip income, so the Inn's 24 employees don't miss having to put their hands out. They also appreciate having a stable income without seasonal fluctuations. Most staff elected to put the salary increase into a retirement fund.

The policy gives the 30-room hotel a unique positioning tool. Mystery shoppers report that service remains excellent and that employees really don't take tips. A small rate increase now balances the higher payroll cost, but customers still perceive the change as a customer-service improvement. When guests are asked on open-ended comment cards what they liked about their hotel stay, the no-tipping policy is the third or fourth most frequent response.

Jump-Starting Customer Service

Shortly after you buy a car from Hayes Brothers in Salt Lake City, the $60-million dealership invites you over for dinner. The sales staff serves up a complete chicken dinner, washed down with Hayes's own brand of bottled water served in a reusable, take-away 20-ounce bottle.

After dinner, customers are given a hands-on demonstration of how to check auto fluid levels plus remarks on proper car maintenance and operation. Participants' cars get off to a good start with coupons for a free 3,000-mile checkup, lube, and oil change. Door prizes are offered for the oldest car, highest-mileage car, greatest number of vehicles purchased from Hayes Brothers, and other categories. Forty percent of new-car buyers attend the events.

Roger Ogden, general manager of the 130-employee dealership, has turned these **educational dinners** into a customer-service and marketing bonanza. Twenty-five percent of customer thank-you notes mention the dinners. Buick National has videotaped the event, and most dealers in the Salt Lake City area have introduced lesser versions, according to Ogden. Since the program began in 1992, service department sales are up 25%. New-car sales are up also, even though Hayes Brothers does little conventional advertising. "It's a lot of fun for customers and employees," says Ogden, "and our bottled water has really taken off. We give it away all the time and are buying it in 1,000-case lots. Research shows that 75% of these bottles are refilled and reused—and they have Hayes Brothers' customer-service number printed right there on the label."

253
IDEA

Better Late Than Never

I sn't it frustrating to rush to a store, only to find yourself staring at a locked door a few minutes after closing time? What's worse is watching employees still working inside. Short of staying open 24 hours, what can a service provider do to ease a frustrated customer's disappointment?

The Lube Stop, a Beachwood, Ohio, chain of 33 quick-oil-change shops, has a late-arrival policy sensitive to the needs of customers who want service and employees anxious to get home. Customers who pull into the lot after closing are greeted by an employee on the spot, thanked for stopping, and given a menu of Lube Stop services on which the employee has written a $3 **discount for the next visit**. Customers are surprised by the added touch, become much friendlier, and no longer argue about the clock being fast. They get a discount to compensate for the inconvenience of coming back, and Lube Stop doesn't lose sales to competitors.

"The late arrival policy doesn't cost much—fewer than 50 of our 37,000 monthly oil changes involve a late-arrival discount," says CeCe Hanacek, vice-president of operations, "but we generate goodwill and look better than the competition."

How Sweet It Is

Customers thirst for an opportunity to buy local products that offer something special," asserts Bill Webster, owner of Haven's Candies, a candy manufacturer, in Portland, Maine.

Here are a few ways Webster creates a **hometown, personalized environment** for the people who buy his handcrafted candies:

- *Tours.* Haven's leads tours of its production facilities and gives school demonstrations. Customers can watch the candy being made through a viewing window. The tour underscores the freshness of the product and develops a presence for Haven's in the community.

- *Discounts.* A new point-of-sale system with a customer database gives a 5% discount to repeat customers. As a side benefit, clerks learn the names of regular customers, so they can greet them by name as they walk in the door.

- *Sample trays.* When a line forms at the cash register, clerks apologize for the wait and encourage customers to try something from the sample tray. The whole atmosphere changes because the customer doesn't feel ignored.

Webster's strategy of focusing on the purchase environment has paid off. Sales have reached $1 million, a 400% increase over eight years.

More Dependable Than Mom

Eve Rubins, general manager of WBLM, "superserves" the loyal listeners of her Portland, Maine, classic-rock station. From a weekly audience of 160,000, Rubins maintains a database of 15,000 core listeners. First into the database are people who rate WBLM favorably on surveys mailed to the target market. Names are added when people call one of the radio shows or mail in "loyal listener" registration forms peeled from the backs of widely distributed bumper stickers.

WBLM **builds its relationship with core listeners by soliciting their programming preferences and offering them preferential services**. Loyal listeners qualify for on-air promotions and giveaways not available to the general audience. Bimonthly newsletters offer additional exclusive chances to win freebies such as concert tickets and vacation getaways. Each loyal listener receives a birthday card personally signed by all WBLM personalities.

Rubins says that "this type of loyalty-linked customer service reinforces the bond between our station and its most actively supportive listeners. Many businesses attempt to use databases to target loyal customers, but they don't commit the time and resources to doing it right. It's hard work, but we've seen its impact grow: WBLM now dominates the 18- to 34-year-old audience." Rubins gets more positive feedback from the birthday card program than any other customer-service activity. One listener wrote: "I can't believe you sent me a birthday card. That was the greatest. My own mother doesn't even send me a card!"

Flattering Frame-Up

Tom Siebel, chairman and CEO of Siebel Systems, based in San Mateo, Calif., wants to make sure his customers are always on his employees' minds. So he **covered the walls of his sales-force-automation software company with customer paraphernalia**. The lobby is plastered with client logos, and the halls are decorated with framed letters and annual reports from clients. What's more, Siebel Systems' conference and training rooms are named after major clients.

In addition to getting employees' attention, the decor yields another payoff. Says Siebel, "Customers walk in and see their logos in the lobby and their names on the conference door—and they know that we value their business."

257
IDEA

Image Building

Who says nice folks finish last? Iris Harrell, based in Menlo Park, Calif., would say that's nonsense: Being thoughtful indirectly accounted for 72% of her $3.5-million remodeling company's revenues last year, most of which came from previous customers and referrals. Harrell spends 70% of her marketing on **low-cost goodwill efforts that encourage repeat business and generate referrals**. For example, two-thirds of the way into kitchen-remodeling projects, Harrell sends customers a handwritten note apologizing for the inconvenience, along with a gift certificate for dinner at a local restaurant. She budgets approximately $1,500 per year for these gift certificates.

Harrell is also smart to remember the potential inconvenience to neighbors. "It's really about creating a positive presence in the community," she says. "Pardon our dust" letters are sent to every resident living near one of her construction sites. The letter asks neighbors to call if noise, trash, or parking problems persist during construction.

Recently, three homeowners who lived on the same street did call. Instead of complaining, they asked Harrell to bid on their own remodeling projects. All three had been referred to her by their neighbors—four past customers of Harrell's.

"How many times have you been in one of the big chain merchandisers and looked all over the place for someone to help you, only to have the person you find tell you that he or she doesn't work in that department? Truly outstanding customer service means that everything you do—and I mean that literally: everything!— revolves around anticipating and meeting your customers' needs. Not yours, the customers'. Period."

DAVID F. RAMACITTI
author of *Do-It-Yourself Marketing*
(AMACOM, 1994)

Birds of a Feather

Make customers feel part of an extended family and you'll generate satisfaction and loyalty. Participants in Boston Duck Tours, a land and water tour of historic Boston, can purchase a pair of bright yellow lips that, when blown into, produce a quacking sound. Tour participants are encouraged to quack as they pass particular sites.

Customers get so caught up in the act of quacking that many of them permanently attach the lips to their key chains and quack whenever they see one of the company's amphibious vehicles. "It's not unusual to see a group of construction workers quacking at tours as they go by," general manager Cindy Brown asserts.

The quacking **ritual brings customers closer together**. When former tourists see others acknowledging a passing tour with a quack, they often strike up a conversation.

Is this company all it's "quacked" up to be? More than 150 pairs of lips are sold each day of the eight-month tour season. Last year, 234,000 people took the tour, and revenues topped $3 million. "During our peak season, which runs from June through August, there are 200 to 250 people waiting in line to buy tickets when we open up the office," says Brown.

IDEA

No More Nickel-and-Diming

Fifteen years ago, Chris Zane, owner of a $1.6-million bicycle shop, in Branford, Conn., **stopped charging customers for anything that cost less than a dollar**. A customer who wants, say, a master link—an inexpensive part that holds the chain together on a child's bike—gets it for free.

"The cost to me is virtually nothing," says Zane. "We're not going to chase the pennies—we're looking at the long-term effect of giving someone a master link. And you should see the look on people's faces." The annual cost for Zane: less than $100. The lifetime benefit: a satisfied, repeat customer.

Thank You, with Milk and Sugar

Joe DePaolis, vice-president of business development for DeCarolis Truck Rental, in Rochester, N.Y., doesn't want to be just another company that rents or leases trucks. "We want to be the person customers call when they need something," says DePaolis.

To help customers put a face to the voice they hear over the phone, DeCarolis began **taking breakfast to customers**. Employees arrive with a breakfast basket filled with a pound of regular coffee, a pound of decaf, creamer, sugar, herbal teas, DeCarolis coffee mugs, and the morning paper. They also bring bagels and cream cheese.

"Customers usually want to thank one of our employees, now that they've met in person, for helping them in the past," says DePaolis. "We pick up sales leads and schedule plant tours that show customers how we can give them clean, trouble-free equipment. If the company is due for a driver safety award—driving one year without a chargeable accident—our safety director uses the breakfast to present a certificate and gift to the driver. A picture of the presentation is printed in our newsletter."

The seven DeCarolis branches bring breakfasts to a total of 260 customers each year. The 30-minute "customer appreciation" breakfasts were initiated after several years of flat sales, and DePaolis credits the program for the steady increase in sales from 6% to 18% over the last three years. "Customer reaction," says DePaolis, "has been dynamite!"

261

IDEA

Primary Care for Customers

Cactus & Tropicals, a $2.2-million Salt Lake City nursery, publishes *Plant Care* tip sheets, makes house calls, and faxes advice to customers with troubled plants. "I have to educate my customers or they come back with dead plants," says Lorraine Miller.

Miller's customers range from the high-flier with the double-parked BMW who "wants a new plant for a dinner party," to the black-thumb gardener who pleads, "Come over and take care of my houseplants." Explains Miller, "If a customer doesn't care, I shut up. When I'm waiting on people, I see what they want."

She **tailors her business to the individual**—no matter how unusual the required service—and is rewarded with an average purchase of $100, which is twice the norm of about $50. During a recent house call on a wilting $1,800 Rhapis palm, Miller explained that the pot was the culprit, and the owner forked over $700 for a more appropriate one.

Are We Having Fun Yet?

When what you do leaves customers cold, you need an icebreaker. "People don't even want to talk about accounting, because it's so boring," says Yvonne Angelo, cofounder and vice-president of SBT Corp., an accounting-software business, in San Rafael, Calif. But when SBT's receptionist came to work dressed up for the Fourth of July, and customers laughed or stopped to talk to her, Angelo knew that she was on to something.

Not every day is a costume party, but now Angelo gives employees at the front desk a **stash of cash to buy yo-yos, candy, and assorted toys**. The result? Laudatory letters from customers spill in faster. "If employees are relaxed and having fun," Angelo explains, "it comes across to our dealers."

Comforts from Head to Toe

People enjoy being comfortable, and they notice when they're not. Here are two businesses that **gain customer gratitude by providing creature comforts**.

&. Byerly's, an upscale supermarket chain, based in Edina, Minn., keeps 10 umbrellas by the exit of each of its 11 stores. When it's raining, customers can grab an extra-large, blue-and-white umbrella emblazoned with the company name, and they return the umbrellas via the drive-through, parcel-pick-up lane. Umbrellas are in hot demand on rainy days—employees have to keep on top of recovering them from the pick-up area. "We do have to replace 30 or more a year," says Art Miller, director of retail operations, "but it's worth it because customers appreciate the service."

&. Claire March, co-owner of Tapestry Tent Designs, in Fort Collins, Colo., travels to nine trade shows a year to sell hand-painted needlepoint products. "The biggest complaint I hear from buyers is that their feet hurt," says March. She invested $225 in an electric foot massager that she puts next to a chair at the front of her booth. "People love it! Buyers remember us from past years and seek us out, especially late in the day." Of course, March makes use of the captive audience. She spends some of the rest time reinforcing relationships with buyers and pointing out items in her display that the customer might not have seen. It's not uncommon for buyers to place an order at the beginning of the day, return in the afternoon for a massage, and place an additional order after they see something new.

What's in a Name

Many of us have walked into dry cleaners or local grocery stores and have been surprised to be greeted by name. Such personal attention can make customers feel important and cared about. Arranging easier ways for your employees to connect with customers can improve their capacity to give superior customer service.

The Midwest Center for Reproductive Health, a fertility clinic in Minneapolis, takes Polaroid photographs of each new client to help its receptionist learn thousands of names. She is usually able to **greet people by name on their second visit**. "Patients are charmed," says Dr. Randle Corfman, Midwest's medical director. "We see them in stressful situations, and the personal connection increases their confidence in our services."

As Much Fun as Pulling Teeth

Knowing that fear and anxiety make many people put off going to the dentist unless they have to, dentists follow stress-reduction protocols, such as working slowly and communicating with anxious patients. McKenna Family Dentistry, in Palo Alto, Calif., has discovered a way to avoid stress in the first place: **distract the client with movies**.

"More than 85% of our customers use the VCR and cordless headset when they need fillings or other longer dental procedures," says Judi McKenna-Edwards, hygienist and office manager. "We have a big selection of kids' videos, hit movies, and TV comedies without the commercials. Customers love the videos—time goes by faster, and they enjoy themselves." The two dentists also like the videos—the distraction relaxes the patients and keeps them still so that the dentist can concentrate on the dental procedure.

Entertainment is also good for business. According to McKenna-Edwards, 98% of new customers are referrals, and many mention the movies. Patients from all over the country—Nevada, Texas, New York, and Boston—regularly visit the practice when they are in town on business. Some even make special trips.

McKenna-Edwards has received one complaint: One patient, with particularly good teeth, is disappointed because he has never been in the chair long enough to see a show.

Waste Not, Want Not

For years, 250-bed Marion General Hospital, in Marion, Ohio, required patients to choose their meals three at a time. If patients were unable to complete their menu forms, they received the default "house tray" for all three meals. Although patient moods and appetites often changed before the food arrived, the meals, once ordered, could not be changed. Uneaten food and complaints piled up.

Carolyn Kile, director of nutrition services, decided to try a **"just-in-time" system**, allowing patients to order their meals one at a time. Now, when tray technicians retrieve meal trays, they present choices for the next meal verbally and take the patient's order. The technicians get to know the patients, learn all meal possibilities for a given patient's diet, and can customize service. Most important, they humanize the hospital's meal service. If a patient isn't in the room when a tray is retrieved, the food tech is usually able to find him or her later and take the order, thereby avoiding the "house tray."

Not only is the "just-in-time" system more patient-friendly, it works well without breaking the budget. Over a one-year period, raw food costs per meal decreased 9%, and labor costs dropped 12%. Eliminating printed menus reduced printing costs 10%.

267
IDEA

Garden of Eden

Wouldn't you like your retail customers to say, "I love that store, I wish I could spend all my time there"? Sandy Hollow Herb Company knows that customer emotions are tied to the store's ambiance. "When people walk into our store, they are overwhelmed by sights, sounds, and smells," says Mickey Robertaccio, owner of this specialty store, in Wilmington, Del. "It's not unusual for a customer to ask, 'Can I bottle this and take it home?'"

Sandy Hollow Herb tries to deliver superior service and generate lasting customer ties by **creating a 30-minute vacation**—an experience, rather than just a shopping trip with relaxing music. Careful thought goes into the intangibles of store design—including sight, sound, and smell—as well as into selecting staff who can create a community feeling. By providing seating in the herb garden, where customers can chat over a free cup of tea, the store becomes a sanctuary. Customers often bring their lunches to eat in the garden and momentarily escape their busy work environments.

According to Robertaccio, creating a customer haven pays off. Up to 400 customers a week visit her store. Many of her regular customers are individuals who initially came to lunch in the garden.

"There's no great mystery to customer satisfaction. We have all been and will continue to be customers, and we know what makes us happy."

JAMES ORR III
chairman and CEO of UNUM Corp.,
in Portland, Maine

268
IDEA

Spare No Expense

It's a little before 8 a.m. at Direct Tire, a Boston-area automotive shop, and the customer, who works in nearby Waltham, Mass., is getting angry. He called ahead of time to make sure he could get a ride to work while the mechanic checked his car's alignment. But now, while the customer's car sits on the lift, there is a problem. The driver who normally ferries passengers to and from work has just called to say his car won't start—and that he'll be there as soon as he can. Owner Barry Steinberg would be happy to give his customer one of his company's loaner cars, but all have been assigned already.

"I called the local taxi company," says Steinberg, "and in five minutes someone arrived and took the guy to his office. The cab fare cost me $17, but can you imagine how many people he's going to tell this story to? It was the best $17 I ever spent."

That, in a nutshell, describes Steinberg's approach to customer service— the **willingness to do whatever it takes to make the customer happy**. If the customer had been forced to wait, he would have cursed the shop instead of praising it. By calling the cab, Steinberg kept his promise, and he did it in a way that the customer will talk about.

Live Your Mission Statement

The mission of Tuffy Auto Centers is "to provide the best automotive service in the industry through a continuous commitment to quality and customer service." Lending the statement real meaning, Tuffy's president, Keenan Moran, brought the message into the shops—to the employees who interacted directly with customers. Then Tuffy held a series of specially designed weekend workshops for its technicians.

Not long afterward, during the holiday season, Art Rott, a Detroit-area Tuffy franchisee, was visited by a woman who needed work done on her car but could not afford the repairs. Rott offered to extend credit, but she managed to borrow the money she needed. When she picked up her car and asked how much she owed, Rott simply handed her the warranty and wished her a Merry Christmas.

When Rott **refused the customer's repeated attempts to pay the bill**, she called the *Detroit Free Press*. A reporter from the newspaper came out to Rott's shop, interviewed him, and ran a feature with his photo. Although he hadn't done the good deed for the publicity, Rott's fulfillment of the company's commitment to customer service was the perfect holiday gift—not only for the grateful customer, but also for the company.

Welcome to Fun City

Orlando-based Signature Flight Support, the largest flight-support operation servicing private and corporate jets in the United States, makes a game out of turning its unhappiest customers around.

For example, a notoriously grumpy pilot landed one day, only to be met by Signature Flight Support executives, who told him that they had created a special day for him. They provided him with a free rental car, gave him a baseball cap and a jacket, and offered him a coupon for lunch at a good restaurant. Their goal? **Make the grump smile**. And he did, from ear to ear.

Your employees should feel that dealing with customers is fun, not a chore. The executives at Signature Flight Support did not view their "customer-improvement" exercise as an obligation, but rather as a valuable opportunity. Because employees were having fun, they were naturally able to create a positive atmosphere—and a service experience—that customers will remember long afterward.

271
IDEA

Collection Made Easier

Michael Cherim's The Green Spot, in Nottingham, N.H., is a small catalog company that sells biological pest-control agents through the mail to gardeners, farmers, greenhouses, and university labs. From the start, Cherim set out to change the atmosphere of distrust between supplier and buyer that often caused payment difficulties. As a service to his customers, Cherim extends each of them a **line of credit**.

"New customers are very surprised—and happy that I show trust in them," Cherim says. For very large orders, however, he usually requires prepayment or personal credit information.

After thousands of billings, Cherim has had to send late notices to fewer than 1% of his accounts, and he turns an average of only one client per year over to a collection agency. Extending credit also helps The Green Spot avoid credit-card fees. Cherim says that although giving credit so easily may seem careless, it treats customers as responsible adults, which translates into a better payment rate than the typical business garners.

The Power to Satisfy

Take a good look at your company's policies to see whether they exist primarily for your own convenience and protection. If they do, consider whether they are really necessary. While a restrictive policy, such as one on product returns, may protect you from the rare individual who is not completely honest, it may unnecessarily annoy many more honest— and loyal—customers.

Bob Tasca Sr., chairman of Tasca Ford, in East Providence, R.I., says his **employees are instructed to serve customers first**. "My people have a blank check to satisfy the customer. That's our company policy. We make the decisions at the lowest level," says Tasca, who admits that sometimes a customer comes in requesting something a bit extreme. For example, a woman wanted a free replacement tire because one punctured six months after she bought her car from Tasca. But he gave the woman a new tire— an approach that no doubt has helped him become a top Ford dealer in customer satisfaction.

"**I**f a company lost 10% of its
inventory to theft, swift action
would be taken to turn the tide.
If a company is losing 10% of its
customers to competitors,
no one might even notice it."

JON ANTON
consultant for the Center for Customer-Driven Quality,
Purdue University, in West Lafayette, Ind.,
and author of *Customer Relationship Management:
Making Hard Decisions with Soft Numbers*
(Prentice-Hall, 1996)

Van Guard

Families are naturally concerned when they entrust their lifelong possessions to a mover. Having a different crew unload at the other end may make economic sense, but customer service can suffer. Customers prefer to deal with the same person throughout the service process, says Richard May, corporate vice-president of sales and marketing for Alexander's Moving and Storage.

The Baltimore-based moving company, whose business consists of 94% corporate customers, uses the same crew to pack, load, transport, and deliver a shipment, instead of delegating portions of the move to another company at the destination site. Customers feel more secure when they know the movers personally—they are more confident that Grandma's rocker will receive the special care requested.

Service-provider continuity also gives the moving company more control over the entire process. Fewer people involved in each move means fewer communication problems. The result is less breakage and fewer claims. Customers notice the difference, says May. They regularly comment on how little damage there was, compared with their previous moves.

Let's Play Tag

Friendly interactions delight customers. A little nudge from management can make it happen.

The Jordan Pond House Restaurant, in Acadia, Maine, creates **name tags** that mention the town where the employee grew up. Customers frequently ask, "How did you end up in Maine?" Dining services manager Daniel Bridgers says this creates the perfect opportunity for a return question, prompting visitors to talk about their own journeys. The conversations add a personal touch that wouldn't otherwise come easily when a staff of 80 serve 1,800 vacationers during the season's peak. "Whenever one of the staff forgets to put on a name tag, a customer is sure to spot it," notes Bridgers. "It becomes a game for customers to see if there is anyone on staff from somewhere they have been."

Down the road at Dublin Gardens, a small, seasonal garden center, in Trenton, Maine, employees wear **big, bright red buttons** that say, "Ask me for a free sample of our delicious fudge." A sign on the counter says the same thing, but sales are higher when employees wear the buttons. Lou Dublin, owner of Dublin Gardens, figures that people hesitate to ask for a freebie unless they know the employee will be receptive. "People have rapport with another person, not a counter," he muses. "The only difficulty is getting employees to wear the buttons when the boss isn't around."

X

"Unhappy customers don't fight—they switch."

JOHN J. FRANCO
former president of Learning International,
in Stamford, Conn.

No Time for Downtime

Many firms wouldn't dream of providing warranty replacement hardware until after the damaged equipment has been returned. But RapidFire Solutions, a $13-million supplier of computerized point-of-sale systems for restaurants, **sends replacement hardware to customers without waiting to receive the defective equipment**.

Standing behind its belief that nonfunctioning equipment is perilously close to a broken promise, RapidFire "cross-ships" replacement hardware to approximately 150 customers per month from its office in Hillsboro, Ore. Duessa Holscher, director of marketing, says the policy reflects a firm commitment to service. Customers depend on RapidFire to be there for them when problems arise.

For example, once a restaurant goes online, it can't afford to be without a working computer system. "We can't fulfill our promise if we pinch pennies on repair service," says Holscher. Maintaining customer trust is critical because two-thirds of RapidFire's sales come from repeat customers. RapidFire customers buy the promise of increased profitability and easier management. At the same time, slow returns and delinquent accounts are kept to a minimum by withholding technical support when necessary.

"The cost of a few late equipment returns and credit holds is minor," notes Holscher, "compared to the goodwill engendered by the policy."

Ask Us Anything

When Patricia Gallup and David Hall launched PC Connection (PCC), in Marlow, N.H., the nation's first mail-order business devoted exclusively to the IBM personal computer, they formed a customer-support staff of two: themselves. They **dispensed pre-, during-, and post-sale information freely to customers**.

Doling out intensive instruction about complex problems shrinks tight mail-order margins even further. Yet, it was standard policy at PCC that even if its customers bought the product from some guy with a pushcart, PCC would support it.

Didn't that mean PCC may have been hand-holding the buyer of a product that another reseller has already squeezed the profit out of? Sure, but how else could this start-up business build volume? The company grew 183% per year doing it. As far as customer-affairs director Peter Haas was concerned, the best call to PCC was one that began, "I bought this somewhere else, but…" And, with that phone call, PCC made itself a new customer.

277
IDEA

The True Cost of Service

Firms subscribing to the goal of continuous improvement try to recognize problems so they can fix them. That's why Diteck Corp., a manufacturer of surge protectors, in Largo, Fla., has created a **separate account to cover customer-service costs** that don't fit within the scope of warranty or operating accounts. The account is named the "policy account" after the firm's policy of taking care of its customers.

Diteck's budget for the policy account is 2% of the standard cost of shipment, but the company will go over budget when needed, says Robert Daugherty, vice-president and general manager. "It doesn't matter if we are right as rain; no customer should think that we don't stand behind our products." The existence of the policy account sends a strong signal to customer-service representatives that they have the leeway needed to satisfy customers.

278
IDEA

Fixed to Stay Fixed

Just because you think you've fixed a problem for a customer doesn't mean the customer is satisfied. That's why Carol Brachman, customer-support manager for Systems Management Specialists (SMS), makes sure that **every customer who reports a problem is called back several days later**. SMS's clients work for companies that have outsourced their data processing and MIS functions to this 580-employee outfit, located in Santa Ana, Calif.

When an SMS technician or help-desk employee resolves a problem, the employee returns a completed-problem ticket to the help desk. Two or three days later, the help desk makes up to two attempts to reach the customer, to ensure that the problem is fully resolved. "Not all employees like the idea of outsourcing services, so as a provider of outsourced services, we feel perception management is crucial," says Brachman. "The extra call-back gives customers another chance to vent and demonstrates our interest in serving them."

Brachman says the callback is more than just a tool to reduce fallout from problems—it's an opportunity to get comprehensive feedback on all aspects of SMS service. During the callback, clients are asked to rate their satisfaction with SMS service on a four-point scale. Open-ended comments are recorded. This information helps SMS improve the perceptions of the client's senior management.

Could the same results be achieved by calling back a small sample of customers? Brachman believes the extra time needed to call everyone is worth the effort. Sampling may give you feedback on your services, Brachman notes, but you won't manage perceptions of individual customers unless you contact them.

279
IDEA

SWAT Team

If responding to customer emergencies disrupts your normal business operations, take note of a solution developed by Western New York Computing Systems (WNYCS), a systems integrator and outsourcing service. This $100-million company, headquartered in Rochester, N.Y., assigned two-thirds of its 90-plus system engineers to account teams and the rest to a pool of unassigned staff.

The account teams handle planned project work with committed deadlines, and the **pool of unassigned staff is available on demand for unexpected problems**. When not responding to emergencies, these staffers attend to activities without imminent deadlines, such as system configuration or non-emergency equipment repair.

"Employees aren't pulled off planned work, so we meet project deadlines more consistently," says Ken Schwartz, vice-president of technical support. The uninterrupted schedule for project work makes it easier to assign employees with needed skills at the right time. The company is also better able to respond to emergencies because people with a broad range of skills can immediately turn their full attention to the problem.

WNYCS's satisfaction survey ratings have improved from an average of 4.2 to 4.6 on a five-point scale, and the reorganization has also increased productivity, notes Schwartz. A higher percentage of available employee time is now spent on billable work.

280
IDEA

Match Their Medium

Hoss's Steak and Sea House, located in Duncansville, Pa., prides itself on its customer orientation, but it was stumped on how to reduce the most frequent complaint on comment cards: The steak wasn't cooked the way the customer wanted it.

Grilling the chef wasn't the answer. According to Kay Cheskey, director of service training, the real problem was variation in customer perception. The kitchen's perception of medium-rare would never match that of every customer. Cheskey's solution: **identify the perception mismatch earlier in the service process**. As soon as a meal is brought to the table, servers are now trained to ask, "Would you like to cut into your steak to see if it's prepared the way you like it?" rather than waiting several minutes before asking, "Is everything okay?"

This small change makes a big difference, according to Cheskey. The sooner a problem is identified, the more likely a customer will be satisfied. Many customers feel uncomfortable complaining about a meal that's been in front of them for several minutes, and if they do, they end up eating a recooked meal after their companions have finished. By asking the question immediately, the server makes it easier to request a change, resulting in the customer's being able to eat recooked food several minutes sooner. This tactic sends a message to guests that the restaurant is serious about customer satisfaction.

"Customer reaction has been positive," says Cheskey. "Guests view it as an added service, not an interruption. A significant number of customers use the comment cards to say 'thanks for asking,' and the number of complaints has dropped."

"Do you know what percentage
of your customers you lose each
year, fully or partially?
The average company loses 20%
of its customers each year,
a very large scrap heap."

JOAN KOOB CANNIE
author of *Turning Lost Customers Into Gold:
the Art of Achieving Zero Defections*
(AMACOM, 1994)

281
IDEA

The Best Things in Life Are(n't) Free

Few companies these days fail to recognize the importance of offering great customer service, but that doesn't mean you have to give it away. Karmak Software, of Carlinville, Ill., abandoned an old-style service policy for one that **asks customers to pay more if they want more support**—and the switch has worked.

Under the old plan, a fixed customer-service charge was tacked onto every sale. Customers treated the add-on as just another component in the software price, and didn't hesitate to call frequently on Karmak's service department to resolve simple problems. Service costs began wrecking the company's bottom line, says Richard Schein, president and CEO of Karmak. "Instead of using the manuals or actually learning the system, people would call us with every minor problem. And we were paying for it, because we guaranteed unlimited consultation after the sale."

Now, customers must sign up in advance for the level of service they want—a set number of calls per month and a surcharge for calls in excess of the contracted number. Schein won't say how profitable customer service has become, but he claims, "It's so great, we doubled the size of the department."

Customer Alert!

Emotions escalate when a customer is forced to call technical support multiple times for an ongoing problem. Frustration increases when someone has to retell the entire problem with each contact, and customer loyalty plummets.

To help customer-service reps deal with repeat calls, many firms use their databases to summarize previous interactions with customers.

RapidFire Solutions, a supplier of restaurant computer systems, goes one step further. This Hillsboro, Ore., firm posts the names of clients experiencing ongoing problems on a white board visible to all support-line employees. This **critical board** tells phone reps which clients need kid-glove treatment. On any given day, three or four of RapidFire's 2,000 customers are listed on the board.

Using the critical board, tech-support reps can instantly identify callers who need understanding and care beyond the usual discussion of solutions to problems. Those listed are to receive extraordinary levels of empathy and service should they call in. Who gets listed on the critical board? It depends on the customer's perception of need, says Barry Barckley, RapidFire's technical support manager. "While no one likes an ongoing problem, some customers have a lower tolerance than others. The critical board lets us know when we need to put on our best shoes and tie."

283
IDEA

The Message Is the Medium

Business writer John Case was used to being put on hold. But this time he was steamed. The reason: He'd encountered a glitch in Quicken, a personal-finance software program, and called Intuit, its publisher, for help. Case expected a lightning-quick response because he had once referred to Intuit as "the last word" in customer service. However, the company was telling customers they'd have to hold for 20 minutes. Ouch!

Suddenly, a familiar voice came on the line. "This is Scott Cook, president of Intuit," said the recorded message. Yes, Cook admitted, the wait was unacceptable. But then he went on to explain why it was happening (an unexpected jump in sales in an already-busy month) and what the company was doing about it (training 80 new support staff as fast as possible). If the caller would leave a message describing the problem, someone from the company would call back promptly.

Of course, Case would have preferred an on-the-spot solution. But like most customers, he understood that companies can't anticipate everything. What's more, in this case, a little **respect for the customer along with accurate information** about the problem made all the difference between a disgruntled customer and an admiring one.

Over-the-Top Customer Service

Pushing the limits of customer service may not be a part of your marketing plan. It's not a tactic—it is a philosophy, a principle, and an attitude that your whole company must share for it to work. And when it works, it can pay off.

Stew Leonard's, a Norwalk, Conn., milk delivery company that grew into a $200-million grocery business, **encourages employees to use initiative to satisfy customers**. One Saturday a woman came in to order $40 worth of food for a lunch party of 20. The chef told her she really should order more, but she resisted. A few hours later the manager got a frantic phone call. "Why didn't you insist I buy more food? I'm going to run out!" The manager put together another $40 tray, drove it over to her house, and apologized. He also refused payment, saying, "No, it's on us."

It turned out the party was for 20 real estate agents new to the area. "Now, what's the first thing someone who's buying a house wants to know? Where's the grocery store!," says Stew Leonard Jr., president of his family's business.

"Right after their party all 20 came down to the store and bought hundreds and hundreds of dollars' worth of food—they all had full shopping carts," recalls Leonard.

285
IDEA

Two-Wheeler Dealer

A **lifetime-service guarantee** is the foundation of Zane's Cycles, in Branford, Conn. "A guy once came in with a six-year-old pump that had worn out," recalls Chris Zane, the shop's owner. "And I just gave him a new one."

Why? Because Zane bets on what each customer's lifetime of business would be worth to his store. And because he has a good relationship with the manufacturer, he knows he can send the broken pump back and get credit, no questions asked.

"The guy has been in twice since then," says Zane. "He's probably spent $200 on accessories." And when it's time for a new bike, Zane expects to get first shot at the sale. At an average cost of $400 for a bike, he stands to make another $140. And a customer who is thrifty enough to have a pump repaired is likely to be so impressed with getting something for nothing that he'll spread the word.

Meanwhile, for a modest $30 investment—the cost of the pump—the business makes a 700% return. That's the kind of know-how that added up to $1.6 million in 1996 sales.

286
IDEA

You Get What You Pay For

Finding the right balance between after-sales support and low prices can be tricky. Great Plains Software, a $57-million developer of accounting software, in Fargo, N.D., manages to satisfy demanding and budget-minded customers by offering a **multitiered support system**: For incremental prices, various levels of after-sale support are available.

The range of services works well for Great Plains Software. While many budget-conscious customers opt for a basic service plan that covers general troubleshooting of software installation and use, others pay more for services such as training, software enhancements, and answers to general accounting and tax questions.

Similar to the multitiered support system is Great Plains' **multitiered response-time guarantee for support calls**. Customers can subscribe to a plan guaranteeing that they will not wait more than one hour for a return call when their initial query isn't answered immediately. A less expensive three-hour response plan is also available. "Our company's record for meeting its guaranteed response time is 249,020 calls in a row," says Scott Lozuaway-McComsey, vice-president of dynamics.

In short, varying the service plan was a great plan for Great Plains. The company's surveys indicate that customers are satisfied with its services—customer satisfaction weighs in at a hefty 4.7 on a five-point scale.

You Won't Wait Forever

Minutes seem like hours to anyone sitting by the phone waiting for an answer to a problem. Time moves even slower for those on hold. Health Benefits America (HBA), a Salt Lake City-based benefits management company, tries to minimize perceived wait time as well as actual wait time. If a question can't be answered immediately, the **customer-service rep commits to a time when the customer will be called back** with an answer.

"Our customers are busy, and each minute they spend on hold is a loss of valuable time," says MaryAnn Holladay, senior vice-president of human resources management, communications, and network management. "By committing to a call-back time, we assure our clients that their issues will be resolved shortly, which allows them to attend to their other business. This diminishes the feeling of waiting and increases satisfaction."

This approach to managing the perception of wait time only works, notes Holladay, if the reps keep their promises. Employees are trained to estimate call-back times and call customers by the promised time, even if only to provide a status report. Call monitoring shows that this is happening. HBA tracks return-call times so employees can better understand what to promise.

288
IDEA

Thermometer Under the Tongue

Smart companies have a plan in place to win back disgruntled customers, and the management company of the Orlando Magic professional sports teams adds an extra dimension to its service-recovery plan. Every complaining customer is categorized as having one of five temperatures: livid, very upset, upset, okay, or calm. **A different complaint management approach is used for each temperature.**

"If a customer is livid, for example, the complaint is immediately directed to a customer-service supervisor or the president of the company," says Jamey Lutz, quality and customer-service specialist. "If the caller seems calm, then any employee is expected to listen empathetically and resolve the issue right then and there."

Customer temperature is included in the complaint tracking process. Lutz tracks the number of complaints by temperature and analyzes which types generate the strongest customer reaction. "The practice of gauging customer temperature has given us greater understanding of the causes of dissatisfaction and has led us to improve our system for satisfying upset customers," says Lutz.

289
IDEA

Cutting a New Deal

Recruiting new customers is expensive. That's why Ron Provenzano, co-owner of $5.2-million Zano's Hair Design, in Naperville, Ill., finds it more profitable to recover lost customers.

Each day Provenzano prints a list of customers who have not visited the salon in four months. Employees call these previous clients to schedule an appointment. **Dissatisfied customers are invited back** for a complimentary cut and style and are also given a multiple-discount voucher to encourage return visits. "Customers are more likely to give you a second chance if they know you are concerned about them and will listen to them," Provenzano says. "If you get customers to come back more than once, they can be yours forever."

The call is worthwhile, even if the customer doesn't return. Zano's uses the call to find out why these people left and which salons they have switched to. "Calling is not always pleasant, but it's an opportunity to learn about what's happening in the business," says Provenzano. The lessons learned help to keep current customers satisfied. "Little extras—offering a cappuccino, giving a neck massage after a stressful day, or walking someone to his or her car under an umbrella when it's raining—make a difference," Provenzano says.

Abolish the Fine Print

Although service contracts provide customers with a certain peace of mind, they can also be a hassle to use. Who has the patience to read the fine print and look for serial numbers during an emergency? "I don't like receiving that type of customer service, and I don't want my customers to have that experience," says Mary Black, owner of a car-wash builder, based in Morrisson, Ill. As a result, Super Wash customers don't buy or receive any service contract—and there is no automated telephone attendant, either.

The **all-inclusive service policy** helps keep car washes in tip-top condition, which is one of the company's best advertisements. "We'd rather help customers with an equipment breakdown and have it repaired properly than have them calling their Uncle Bob to jerry-rig a solution," says Black. Super Wash will also answer any question customers have relating to their car washes. "Why? Because 50% of car washes sold are bought by existing customers."

Lemon Aid

Many customers feel cheated if a product breaks shortly after the warranty expires. How can businesses overcome customer suspicions that the warranty was designed to run out before problems arose?

Intech Construction, in Philadelphia, has found a way to avoid warranty woes. One month before the warranty expires, the team that completed the project formally inspects it with the customer. If additional work is needed, it can be completed within the warranty period.

The proactive inspection reassures clients that Intech conscientiously builds to contracted specifications. Subcontractors know of the inspection, which is an additional incentive for them to do the work properly. "Our inspection shows that we deliver what we sell," says Louis Parise, vice-president of operations for the 50-person construction company. Intech **extends its commitment to customers beyond the warranty period** when the work needed is covered by the spirit of the warranty.

"Our goal is repeat business," adds Parise, "so customer satisfaction is our top priority. One customer alone has returned for 53 projects in 10 years."

292

IDEA

Oil on Troubled Waters

Phone calls from irate customers needn't be adversarial, emphasizes Lou Woodson, director of training for Unitel Corp., a $20-million provider of outsourced telemarketing, customer service, and fulfillment services, in McLean, Va. Here are four of Woodson's **tips for defusing angry customers**.

- *Empathize and express regret that the customer is upset.* Say, "I understand this was frustrating for you, Mr. Jones, and I'm sorry you feel this way." You aren't admitting fault, but you are on your way to earning the customer's cooperation.

- *Be frank about what you want.* After listening to the problem, state your desired outcome: "We want to resolve this problem, and we want you to continue as our customer."

- *Gently correct mistaken perceptions without confronting the customer.* If the customer feels that an offer was misrepresented in a direct-mail letter, explain that you make every effort to present offers clearly, and ask where the recipient thinks the miscommunication occurred. When customers reread the letter, they usually discover their own mistake without you having to say "You're wrong."

- *Make the caller feel like a winner.* Ask, "How would you like the problem solved?" Provide what the caller wants, and promise to follow through. Let people know they are important by saying, "Ms. Jones, I'm glad you called. It's customers like you who help us improve. Thank you for the opportunity to make it right."

293

IDEA

Saying "No" Is a "No-No"

How many customers have you lost because your customer-service reps say "no" to a request? "Too many" was the conclusion reached by ECCO, a manufacturer of safety warning devices, in Boise, Idaho.

Service people may be trying to be careful with the company's money, but the unintentional result may be a lost order or an angry customer complaining to management. So ECCO instituted a new policy for service reps: **If you are tempted to say "no," see a supervisor first**.

"Most firms do it the other way around, requiring permission to spend money," says Dan McCann, ECCO's sales manager. "Our philosophy is, there's nothing you can do that we can't fix. If a customer asks a service rep to send something by next-day air, it should be done, and we'll review the situation later to see if we should change the stock arrangement for that customer."

ECCO encourages its staff to accept all warranty requests. If an after-the-fact assessment reveals that the customer used the wrong product, then the company's field staff will propose a product that works better for that application. "We view the expense as an investment in our customer and in future business," says McCann.

Are the service reps making the right judgment calls? When the reps resolve problems on their own, they do the right thing almost 100% of the time, says McCann. When they can't figure out a way to fix the problem, the supervisor almost always can.

A Graceful Goodbye

You undoubtedly give good service to new and current customers, but how do you treat the ones who are switching to your competitor? If you **treat exiting customers right** and leave them with a positive impression, you may eventually win them back.

"When customers choose not to renew their contracts, we make sure we finish with 100% service or more," says Dave Pasek, president of Service Performance Corp., a San Jose, Calif., janitorial company with 1,000 employees. Supervisors and account managers continue their client communications and weekly walk-through inspections, and the company coordinates with its successor to ensure a smooth transition. "It's a small business community, so reputation is important," says Pasek. One customer, who selected a lower bid, retracted the cancellation after realizing that the future replacement company wasn't showing the same level of interest. Pasek points out that it's hard for customers to admit they made a mistake by canceling because of price. Finishing the job with exceptional performance makes it easier for them to come back a year or two later.

The John Akridge Companies, a real-estate business, in Washington, D.C., sends potted plants to customers who relocate their offices to other commercial office developments. "Exit interviews indicate that customers are pleased with our services but choose new facilities to meet their expansion needs," says Amy McBroom, director of communication. "Our gift is a token of our appreciation for their business and serves as a permanent reminder of our high level of service. We've had customers return to our properties because they haven't received the same level of service elsewhere."

Long-Term Commitment

As much as Dan McNulty, president and CEO of Acoustic Imaging Technologies, in Tempe, Ariz., tried to convince prospects about his diagnostic ultrasound equipment's reliability, they wouldn't listen. So he juiced up the product's one-year warranty to make prospects prick up their ears. If the $130,000 machine broke down and was unusable, they received an automatic one-year **warranty extension from the date of the breakdown**, at no charge. "It differentiates us from our competitors, with whom one-year warranties are the standard," says McNulty.

Since the program was introduced, McNulty claims the company is ahead of sales projections. And only one customer has been able to take advantage of the extension, which normally sells for $10,000.

Proactive Satisfaction

How do you keep customers satisfied when a product may have a significant defect? Be proactive. **Inform them of potential problems and give them options**. A.G. Findings and Manufacturing Company, a maker of beeper accessories, in Sunrise, Fla., does just that. Company policy states that whenever a problem is discovered with a product, all customers are contacted and informed about the potential defect. They are given choices: 1) keep the product and wait to see if a problem develops; 2) send it back to be checked and repaired, if necessary; or 3) return it for replacement free of charge. All shipping costs are absorbed by the company.

Marketing director Elena Van Scoyoc asserts, "Customers are surprised when we call to alert them to the possibility of a defect. Although such calls are infrequent, they derive great satisfaction from the fact that we've let them know about the problem, given them options for resolving it, and charged them nothing. Even if the item they have isn't defective, they love knowing we stand behind our products." Customers love it so much that this company has become a local market leader with more than 6,000 customers.

297

IDEA

We're All Ears

Listening comes naturally when talking with a friend over lunch, but not when employees talk on the phone," observes Al Jacquez, manager of training and development for AFFINA Corp., a Troy, Mich., supplier of comprehensive marketing services. "We train our call-center representatives to listen aggressively. Listening well is an active practice, not something that just happens." Jacquez offers a few **tips for listening and responding to customers**.

- *Let people vent.* Resist the urge to step in with a solution. They need to tell their whole story and will resent an interruption.

- *Use open probes to gather general information* ("Can you tell me what happened?"), and follow up with direct probes ("Tell me more about the promise he made."). Angry people rarely communicate clearly, so ask pointed questions to get clarification.

- *Use reflective probes* ("Let me make sure I understand. You...'"). Paraphrasing what they said gives people a chance to correct misunderstandings and add details not mentioned the first time. It also proves that you are listening.

- *Stay in the moment.* Don't get so caught up in thinking about your response that you tune the customer out. Listen to every word and take notes.

- *Use "I" rather than "we."* The customer doesn't connect with a generic group of people. You are the company.

- *Don't talk about other departments as "they" and blame them.* The customer sees the company as one big team. Blaming is a waste of time—it doesn't defuse anyone or solve the problem.

298
IDEA

Preventive Maintenance

Smart car owners make sure their cars get routine checkups. They rarely do the same for their fine antiques, which may be more valuable than the family car. Michael Corbett provides this service for them at Federalist Antiques, a Kenilworth, Ill., store specializing in the sale of furniture and accessories from the American Federal period.

Several years after a sale, he **offers certain customers a free consultation** with a professional furniture restorer in the customer's home. The one-hour house call provides an opportunity for the restorer to touch up finishes, make minor adjustments, and identify other problems before they become serious. The restorer may move a fine oil painting hanging directly above a steam radiator or put a leveling shim under an armoire to prevent the doors from binding. When more serious problems are detected, customers may arrange with Corbett to have the work done, or they can make their own arrangements.

House calls do more than protect antiques. Corbett educates customers about the historical use of the pieces he sells and advises about the best possible uses for them in the home. He has also resold furniture that customers no longer need. The visits, Corbett says, keep him in touch with good customers and with the antiques he has sold.

Red Alert

Some people, it seems, you just can't please. But Neil Cannon will die trying. Cannon, chairman and CEO of Schmidt-Cannon International, a distributor of promotional products, headquartered in Ontario, Calif., has developed a **problem-customer order tracking system**.

Cannon is convinced that customers most prone to complaining are those who have filed grievances already. So any time the company receives a complaint, that customer's next order gets placed in a red file folder for special attention. As the folder is passed through departments, each manager personally signs off on it. If a problem arises, the manager responsible speaks directly with the customer. Since the system was introduced, there has been a noticeable drop in repeat complaints.

Quarterly Check-up

It pays to know your customers' needs and how they view your service. What's the best way to find out? John Gunther, owner of Bucks vs Bytes, a full-service computer consulting firm, located in Rosendale, N.Y., devised a system of phone calls that sheds light on both.

Every three months or so, Gunther **calls to check his customers' pulse**. They may not want anything new, he notes, but a lot of times they have two or three things that need work. Gunther might find a monitor that needs adjusting or a network that's not functioning properly. "My call prompts them to fix the problem. Each time it's a few hundred dollars for me. And once in a while someone says, 'While you're here, I hired a new employee and I need another computer.' Clients get the feeling that my company is always there for them," Gunther says. "It makes them feel we're a partner who cares about their business."

Gunther also has a quality-control employee contact clients a few weeks after each job. "I deal with most of the customers directly," he explains. "They usually won't tell me if they're unhappy with something. So, I have another person call. One customer I know well complained that I was late, which forced him to change his dinner plans. He didn't say anything to me, but it was worth knowing that he was upset."

301

IDEA

No Service, No Sale

Turning down a sale is tough. After all, selling is what salespeople are trained and paid to do. But, if Multiplex can't provide foreign customers in remote locations with reliable 24-hour service for repairs of its automatic beverage dispensers, that's exactly what it does. "It's easy to sell and forget," says J.W. Kisling, CEO of the St. Louis-based company. "But broken-down equipment can badly damage a company's reputation. We saw an opportunity to compete by providing customers with service, and we've made that our niche."

To provide **reliable service in unfamiliar territories**, Multiplex contacts maintenance managers of major hotel chains that have established outlets in the area, and it asks them for recommendations of local repair services. Multiplex then checks the literacy rate of the company's employees, in addition to its financial stability and reputation for emergency repairs. "In developing countries like Nepal or Africa, where literacy rates are low and there aren't many refrigerators, finding someone who can read the manuals and has the proper experience is a priority for us," adds Mark Suddarth, international marketing manager for Multiplex.

• INDEX • INDEX •

3O1
GREAT
CUSTOMER SERVICE
IDEAS

• INDEX • INDEX •

Other business books from *Inc.* magazine

HOW TO *REALLY* CREATE A SUCCESSFUL BUSINESS PLAN
HOW TO *REALLY* CREATE A SUCCESSFUL MARKETING PLAN
HOW TO *REALLY* START YOUR OWN BUSINESS
By David E. Gumpert

MANAGING PEOPLE
HOW TO *REALLY* RECRUIT, MOTIVATE, AND LEAD YOUR TEAM
Edited by Ruth G. Newman

HOW TO *REALLY* DELIVER SUPERIOR CUSTOMER SERVICE
Edited by John Halbrooks

THE SERVICE BUSINESS PLANNING GUIDE
THE RETAIL BUSINESS PLANNING GUIDE
By Warren G. Purdy

ANATOMY OF A START-UP
WHY SOME NEW BUSINESSES SUCCEED AND OTHERS FAIL:
27 REAL-LIFE CASE STUDIES
Edited by Elizabeth K. Longsworth

MANAGING PEOPLE: 101 PROVEN IDEAS FOR MAKING YOU
AND YOUR PEOPLE MORE PRODUCTIVE
FROM AMERICA'S SMARTEST SMALL COMPANIES
Edited by Sara P. Noble

301 GREAT MANAGEMENT IDEAS
FROM AMERICA'S MOST INNOVATIVE SMALL COMPANIES
Edited by Leslie Brokaw
with Bradford W. Ketchum, Jr.

301 DO-IT-YOURSELF MARKETING IDEAS
FROM AMERICA'S MOST INNOVATIVE SMALL COMPANIES
Edited by Sam Decker

www.inc.com/products

To receive a complete listing of *Inc.* business
books and videos, please call 1-800-468-
0800, ext. 5505. Or write to *Inc.* Business
Resources, P.O. Box 1365, Dept. 5493,
Wilkes-Barre, PA 18703-1365.